MW01489757

SILENCE IN HEAVEN

A STUDY OF REVELATION 8:1

D. ROBERT KENNEDY Ed.D, Ph.D.

PRINTED IN THE UNITED STATES OF AMERICA

2001 02 03 04 05 06 07 08 09 10 · 5 4 3 2 1

The author assumes full responsibility for the accuracy of all facts and quotations as cited in this book.

ISBN 1-57258-208-1
Library of Congress Catalog Card No. 2001092642

Unless otherwise noted, Bible texts in this book are from the Holy Bible, New Revised Standard Version © 1991 by the Division of Christian Education of the National Council of Churches of Christ in the United State of America.

A few Bible texts have been freely translated by me, but every effort has been made not to do violence to their meaning.

Cover design by Leighton Kennedy

Published by

TEACH Services, Inc.
254 Donovan Road
Brushton, New York 12916

DEDICATED

To all who have confronted the symbol of the heavenly silence and the silences of this world. It is my wish that you might grow in faith, hope and love and that together we can share the ecstasy of the heavenly Sabbath silence.

CONTENTS

ACKNOWLEDGEMENTS

If there were no one to listen to us, acknowledging what we say and do, all of us would be reduced to silence. Therefore in this venture, I acknowledge those who have taken the time to hear my absurdities and the brief flashes of my wisdom. In dealing with a subject as complex as the heavenly silence, I have been led to reference many authors and need to thank them, but nothing is so helpful as having someone with whom you can dialogue. R. Dean Davis, the Chair of my Religion Department provided the latter. His understanding of the issues in Revelation is profound and he has been very kind in sharing such understanding with me. I thank the Atlantic Union College Theology Honor Society for having allowed me the privilege of presenting my introductory chapter to them. It was such a presentation that gave me the chance to clarify my thesis and focus on the contextual and methodological issues that were of highest import. I am grateful to my wife, June, who has had to suffer with the fleshing out of my new ideas whenever I work at a subject. She has ever been a great encourager. She receives much credit for my completing the study. Other persons such as Jeanette Bryson, Dr. Ann Parrish, Carol Brown, Karen Silverthorn, and Dr. Rollin Shoemaker who helped me to see dimensions of silence that I had not seen, must receive my gratitude. Greatest thanks to Dr. Ray Parker, my colleague and friend at Trinity Seminary, for his constant encouragement about the direction that I have taken. I also thank many other unnamed persons who have helped me along the way of this challenging study.

Whatever limitations are inherent in this work are mine and only mine. What I hope, however, is that what I have presented will not only be seen as an attempt to fulfill the requirements of a course of study or to provide some knowledge, but will serve as a document of faith assurance. This is of greatest significance to me because there are millions of persons in our world who are reduced to silence by satanic oppression (the dumb, the deaf, the sick, the abused, and the persecuted). What I wish then that they would know is that some day when God speaks his last word they will be able to speak many words. They will share in the glory of heaven where their deadly silence in life will be broken.

PREFACE

The phenomenon of the half-an-hour of heavenly silence found in Revelation 8:1 is one of the most challenging themes in the book of Revelation and all of Scripture. The study examines the symbolic and metaphoric meanings of this silence and takes note of its impact on human lives in general, and the faith experience of God's people in particular. Although it recognizes that the phenomenon of silence is hard for us to grasp in a human frame, because silence is on the boundary of human communication, it contends that God does not always speak and must not be always expected to speak.

With the understanding that the phenomenon of silence is such a challenging reality of all of life, the methodology used in this study is biblical, theological, philosophical, and psycho-social.[1] Only by following all of these directions can we enter into the uncertainties of the whispers that come forth from the heavenly silence. One might find it hard to hear one speaking with a lisp about the way to study this silence, but this is what a theme like this does to a person. It sets a person on roundabouts, and lets the person pay keen attention to what is to be heard from many directions at a time. So while I seek textual understanding, I also find a place for the inner search that is pursued in time and silence. In effect, one who studies a time of silence in any frame has to listen with keenness to multiple streams of thoughts. Time is mysterious and silence is mysterious. Both issues raise many questions for us.

---

[1] See Carl Jung (1954), Answer to Job: The Problem of Evil: Its Psychological and Religious Origins (Cleveland Ohio: The World Publishing Company), in which Jung tries to bring a psychoanalytic interpretation to the Apocalypse. He suggests that its collective and archetypical nature directs us to the very personal situation of the prophet.

Some of the questions raised in the study follow the direction of those asked, in limited ways, by a multitude of other scholars. But this study seeks to examine such questions more extensively. It puts forward the question: Is the half-an-hour of silence that John uses to connect his discussion of the seals to other issues just a rhetorical device within the frame of Revelation or is there some theological, philosophical and psychological justification for this silence? It argues that perhaps we are dealing with a phenomenon that has to do with the divine response to the prayers of the saints, or the great eschatological judgment of God and the Second Coming of Christ. Does the silence mean that God will not speak at the end of the judgment? Does it mean that heaven will be emptied of its host when Christ is on His way to earth? What does it say about these questions, for it is understood that the deepest truths do not always find their way through verbal expressions.[2] My greatest concern has focused on the question of whether this time of silence means that God has abandoned His people at the end or whether He is still speaking to them through His providential power. In effect, we ask consistently, what of the silence for the faith of the people of God? And how does it lead them to live their lives in the world?

After posing the foregoing questions as a point of departure, I have organized this study in five basic sections. In section one I note the contextual question surrounding the half-an-hour of silence in Revelation 8:1. In section two I consider the challenge of understanding heaven as a place of silence when the descriptions we get from John in Revelation and Scripture in general are that heaven is a place of constant sound and activity. In section three I expand the issue begun in section two, which notes that God is the God who speaks from heaven. Here we conclude that God is free to speak and God can be silent and when

---

[2] Abraham J. Heschel (1955), God in Search of Man: A Philosophy of Judaism (New York: Farrar, Straus and Giroux), 95.

God is silent it can lead to faith as well as to apostasy. In the fourth section I suggest that when God is silent it often means that God is bringing His judgment on humanity. His judgment is one of warning, rebuke, vindication, and retribution. The people of earth are warned and rebuked. If they accept the mercy of God they will be brought to salvation, but if they refuse to accept judgments of warning they will be destroyed by the wrath of God. God has chosen to speak to vindicate His name and His people, but He does not have to speak. In both speech and silence He is vindicated. Here I posit that often enough the wicked trivialize the silence of God, thinking that God does not see them and that God does not care to get involved in our human interest. Some have even made claims to the effect that God is "dead beyond recall."[3] But such assertions are blown apart when God comes and begins to speak again. In the final section I look at what the silence means for the people of God, for this silence is their last great temptation. While they are waiting for God to speak they will become profoundly anxious, but does this anxiety lead them to apostasy or to a more profound trust in God? I contend that silence leads to a deepened faith. Such issues as the time of waiting for the second coming, the time of the resurrection of the righteous, the time of the eternal Sabbath rest, the time of the assurance of meeting the Divine Lover, are affirmations of the faith of God's people. The half-an-hour of heavenly silence is that which connects all despair to hope, all judgments to the promise of salvation, all bondage to the freedom of God, all times of suffering to the time of rejoicing, and the *Deus abscunditus* to the *Deus manifestatio*. Out of the night of the deafening time of silence comes the beautiful morning of the eternal manifestation. In the reality of eternity God is in the most intimate communication with humanity.

---

[3] John A. T. Hamilton (1963), Honest to God (Philadelphia: Westminster Press), 180.

I

SILENCE IN HEAVEN: A STUDY OF REVELATION 8:1

Listening for heavenly sounds

For quite a few years now astronomical scientists at the Harvard University observatory and other observatories around the world have been using state-of-the-art telescopes to listen to heavenly sounds. Their goals, however, are far beyond the gathering of data. They are using their knowledge of radio astronomy to listen for the sound of intelligent life from outer space. Their wait has been long, but as the new millennium presses forward, expectations of connecting with other intelligences in the universe heighten, for it is the assumption of a great number of individuals that there is life on planets other than the earth. Indeed, in recent years, Radio Astronomy has become one of the most popular contemporary sciences. Since 1932 when radio astronomy was first discovered, many projects have been established to carefully examine outer space and to listen with extremely sensitive receivers to sounds from non-natural sources.[4]

---

[4] Cf. "Educators guide to life beyond earth," on the Internet. Much information on the use of High Resolution Microwave Survey (HRMS) can be found through the Jet Propulsion Laboratory Public Education Office, Oak Grove Drive, Pasadena. These scientists say that their search for extraterrestrial intelligence

I have heard someone state that since technology has encircled the earth, there is a belief that silence and isolation are banished. It is no wonder that as the Hale Bopp comet was about to appear (between March 23-25, 1997), and millennial (chiliastic) fever intensified, that thirty-nine people belonging to the Heaven's Gate cult, who were listening for sounds from heaven, took their lives. As the group's leader, Marshall Applewhite, blended computer technology and biblical prophecy along with astrology and New Age concepts and shared his views, the group came to believe that after dying they would rise from the dead and ascend to heaven in a cloud. The cloud was to be a spacecraft that would transport them as the elect to heaven. With the coming of the Hale Bopp comet, their views coalesced and they prepared for their heavenly transport on the tail of the comet. One will never know whether they heard any voices, but it was discovered after their death that they had been very involved in the best of contemporary sound communication.[5] My own feeling is that they did not hear a word from heaven. In their psychotic condition, I believe, they heard a message that forced itself upon their minds, telling them: "Kill yourselves." This may be a prejudiced perspective that might require further discussion. The point, which is noted in both biblical and contemporary experience, is that life is sad and quite insane when heaven seems to be silent. When people hear heavenly sounds it seems to inspire hope in their breasts, and when there are no sounds they seem to be filled with anxiety and despair. These are days when people are claiming to be hearing voices from

---

(SETI) is not a wide-eyed search for "aliens" like that reported in supermarket tabloids. Rather it is a search for life that might exist on planets thousands of light years away. This would mean that a sound emitted from any planet in a far away galaxy could take fifty to a hundred years to reach us.

[5] . Cf. Jean Bethke Elshtain, "The Hard Questions: Heaven Can Wait," *The New Republic* (May 5, 1997), 23; Stephen Hedges, "How an Obscure Cult Mixed Computers, UFOs, and New Age Theology so its 39 Members Could Take the Ultimate Journey," *U.S. News and World Report* (April 7, 1997), 25-28.

everywhere. Channelers are saying that the Gaian biota is speaking to us and tolerance demands that we must listen to it, and accept it.

The ambiguity of silence and the question in Revelation 8:1

Listening for heavenly sounds has been one of the preoccupations of humanity since the dawn of time.[6] It does not seem a strange thing when Adam and Eve hear the "sound" of the Lord walking in the Garden at the time of the evening breeze (Gen 3:8). Nor was it a surprise when Cain had to answer for the death of his brother Abel (Gen 4:9-11). Even though there has been at times an evident disinterest in heavenly sounds, still heaven remains the place that most persons hope to reach someday.[7] It is of significance therefore that an attempt to understand the heavenly sounds and silence should lead us to Revelation 8:1 "When he opened the seventh seal, there was silence in heaven for about half an hour." Here the problem of silence (Gk. *sige*) is presented. Max Picard says, sometimes silence exists without speech, but speech never exists without silence.[8] So what of the heavenly silence? Is the heavenly silence different from what humanity knows as silence? Is God's silence different from human silence? J. E. Seiss says that this silence has made a good deal of noise in the world, especially among commentators. And it has been difficult to find another point upon which there has been so many different and discordant voices. He also notes that one commentator even gives it as a general rule that when expositors come to this silence they break out into all sorts of contradictory conjectures. For although the

---

[6] In wind, thunder, storm, earthquake, spoken word, epiphanic and theophanic appearances humanity listened for the voice of the Lord. (Cf. Ex 19-20; 1 Kings 19:9-18; Isa 29:6).

[7] See Dave Hunt (1988), Whatever Happened to Heaven? (Eugene, Oregon: Harvest House).

[8] Max Picard (1952), The World of Silence (Chicago: H. Regency), 13.

marks of historic continuity are as distinct as it is possible to make them, some take this silence as a full stop to the chain of apocalyptic predictions, and so treat what follows as a mere reiteration, in another form, of what already preceded it. Others regard it as a blank, leaving everything belonging to the seventh seal unrevealed, so that its action can only be known when we come to the immortal life. Some pronounce it a mere poetic invention to heighten the dramatic effect, but having no particular significance. Others treat it as a prophetic symbol of scenes and experiences in the earthly history of man: some, as the suspension of divine wrath in the destruction of Jerusalem in ACE 70; some as the interval of repose enjoyed by Christians between the persecutions by Domitian in ACE 80s and Galerius in ACE 311 and the beginning of the civil wars toward the end of the latter year; some as the disappearance of human striving against God and His Christ; others as a lull in earthly revolt and the millennium of peace and righteousness to be induced by the triumphs of rest of the saints.[9]

David Grey Barnhouse comments thus:

> What is the meaning of the silence of God? Perhaps we may come to the answer as we survey the revelation of God from the Old Testament through to this last Word. Perhaps the explanation is that the silence in Heaven is occasioned by the end of what in the Old Testament, has been called the silence of God. Throughout the Old Testament, the men of God cried out against the seeming triumph of evil. The Spirit of God gave the answer through David, "Our God shall come, and shall not keep silence: a fire shall devour before him, and it shall be very tempestuous round about him. He shall call to the heavens from above, and to the earth, that he may judge his people"(Ps.50: 3,4). The

[9] J. A. Seiss (1981), The Apocalypse Lectures on the Book of Revelation (Grand Rapids, Michigan: Zondervan), 180, 181.

prophet's view was, of course, that God was going to bring righteousness and judgment to the earth, but buried in the midst of unrighteousness their impatient souls cried, "How long shall the wicked triumph?" (Ps. 94:3). They "inquired and searched diligently...searching what, or what manner of time, the Spirit of Christ which was in them did signify, when it testified beforehand the sufferings of Christ, and the glory that should follow"(1Pet. 1:10,11). There is an eager desire in heaven and on earth to know when God will break his silence and effectively end the ills of earth.[10]

There are multiple words for silence in the Old and New Testaments, and they carry a variety of nuances. When reference is made, for example, to one who is deaf or dumb, a note is made of silence (Heb. *Haras*, Gk. *Kophos*). When one who is capable of speech refuses to speak (Heb. Hasa, Gk. sigao), such as when God refuses to speak or act or to pay attention (Heb. *Sakat*, cf. Psa 35:22), this is also noted as silence. And when there is reflection on God's quietness (Heb. *Dumah,* Gk. *sige*) bcfore God breaks out in judgment, it is also noted that there is silence. Truly, silence, as a general phenomenon, is a challenging thing. At the end of history when God will speak out of silence as in the beginning when He spoke and things were done, He commanded and things stood fast, the challenge will be evident. Thus "How shall we contemplate the issue of the heavenly silence, which is noted in one of the most challenging little cryptic texts in scripture?"

---

[10] David Grey Barnhouse (1971), Revelation: An Expository Commentary (Grand Rapids, Michigan: Zondervan), 154, 155.

The heavenly silence in the context of the worship, the seals and the judgment in Revelation

Gill Abery says, "The richest texts are dark and obscure."[11] Thus in order to direct our focus we need to look at the textual context to see the symbolic and metaphoric meanings, as John records them. What we see is that the silence of Revelation 8:1 is set in the context of the seals and in the context of worship and judgment. This, we believe, gives it a multivalent sense. When one reads the philosophical works of individuals such as Martin Heideggar, Maurice Meleau-Ponty, Edmund Husserl, and Bernard Dauenhauer, one notes the many valences of silence. I am not interested in reviewing their works here, but I shall draw from their perspectives at many points to ask the special significance of the silence we are pursuing. Each of the above confesses that silence retains a certain level of opaqueness.[12] Such opaqueness is added to when one confronts the fact that heaven is silent for *half an hour*.

The heavenly noises of Revelation have profound interest for Christians, especially as they focus on liturgical sounds, because a large group of Christians have little understanding of any deep silence in heaven or earth. In some Protestant traditions musicians play while the Prayer prays. There is little notion of the mystery of silence. For a great part of the Christian community, the silence of the liturgy is very challenging. Among Christians only Catholics and Quakers employ silence to a high degree, and in Catholic liturgy silence does not reach the obvious and explicit ontological level that it has attained in Quaker worship.[13] A lot

---

[11] Gil Abery "The Silence of God: A Reminiscence about Isaac Bashevis Singer," Tikkuen 9:3 (Jan-Feb, 1994), 61-63.

[12] Bernard P Dausenhauer (1980), Silence: The Phenomenon and its Significance (Bloomington: Indiana University Press), 17.

[13] Ibid, 18.

can be learned about the struggle with silence between the two traditions named as one reads the works of Thomas Merton, the Trappist monk, the Quaker turned Catholic. Merton had studied silence in the Western tradition, but Thomas Omera says that while Merton was faithful to his vow by remaining at his monastery in Kentucky, in 1968 he received permission to accept an invitation to speak in a conference on Catholic monasteries of women and men in Asia. Before the conference he took the opportunity to visit Buddhist hermits and monks, particularly in Northern India. His *Asian Journal* records the impact of his visitation. While he did not convert to Buddhism, he became a Zen sympathizer. He thus began to utilize many Zen (Buddhist) principles relating to silence, prayer, the inner life of contemplation and meditation. On returning home Merton argued that through silence God is moving in all human beings. He also said that silence brings us to the core of all religions. For the latter part of his life, Merton reflected upon silence with a trans-cultural, trans-formational, and trans-religious understanding.[14] What is said to be common to ritual worship in those religions that practice silence is the expectation that God works in the space of silence the worshipers hold open.[15] I shall return at some time to comment on Merton and the helpfulness of understanding silence in various human cultures. Here, I return to my interest which is to examine the meaning of the heavenly silence as it confronts us in Revelation 8:1 and as it is set to impact the faith experience of the people of God, especially in the generation of earth's history.[16]

---

[14] Leo J. O'Donovan and Howland T. Sanks, eds. (1989), Faithful Witness: Foundations of Theology for Today's Church (New York: Crossroads), 162-166. Cf. John F. Teaban, "The Place of Silence in Thomas Merton's Life and Thought," The Message of Thomas Merton, Patrick Hart, ed.

[15] Bernard P. Dausenhauer (1980), Silence: The Phenomenon and its Significance (Bloomington: Indiana University Press), 19.

[16] Renita J. Weems (1999), Listening for God: A Minister's Journey Through Silence and Doubt (New York: Simon & Schuster), 191.

Silence and the seventh seal

To understand the silence from the perspective of Revelation 8:1, I sifted through the many traditions of interpretations that have been used to focus on the text. One interpretation notes, "When the seventh seal was opened there was an arrest of the praises and thanksgiving in heaven . . . in order that the prayers of the suffering saints on earth might be heard before the throne of God."[17] Another interpretation follows the suggestion that: The opening of the seventh seal is recorded in practically the same words that were used in connection with the other six. The book of the prophecies and their certain fulfillment by the Lamb are now completely unsealed. The silence that lasts for about one half-hour is the hushed expectation of all as the removal of this last seal is now undertaken. The silence is in strongest contrast to the tremendous acclaim of the preceding vision, verses 7, 10, 12. No one even speaks, as did the elder to John 7:13-17. "About one half hour" is not a symbolical length of time but only an impressive length for John for whom all else in these visions is intended. The contents of the other seals are not ushered in with this impressiveness, for what this last seal uncovers is something that has not been revealed in earlier prophecies of Scripture as the contents of the first six seals have been.[18]

By the intervening silence in the seventh seal, the simple flow of words or actions is stopped. But the silence is not the end of divine speech and actions. The silence only terminates one series of utterances and actions and opens the way for others. The silence gives expressive force to what has gone before and to what will come after. In effect, silence spurs our anticipation and

---

[17] R.H. Charles (1920), A Critical and Exegetical Commentary on the Revelation of St. John, ICC. (Edinburgh: T & T Clark), 223.
[18] R.C.H Lenski (1957), The Interpretation of St. John's Revelation, (Columbus, OH: The Watburg Press.

alerts us to the surprising things that are about to take place.[19] As Barnhouse says:

> The seventh seal is not a judgment; it is a new beginning. From it come forth seven messengers, each with trumpets to sound further judgments. The word of Christ has been vindicated: "All these are the beginning of sorrows" (Mat. 24:8). We can understand this development by a simple illustration. We have all seen firework displays in which giant rockets are shot into the air exploding into a great ball of fire. This, as it falls toward the earth, bursts again into smaller balls of various colors. So it is with the judgments of God. At first we see nothing but a sealed scroll. As the seals are removed each one appears to be a judgment and we would expect that when we come to the last seal, it would be the last judgment. But instead, the last seal discloses seven angels, each with trumpets. These, in turn, are various judgments, and the seventh trumpet, in turn, reveals not another single judgment, but seven vials of the wrath of God. In both instances there is a series of seven with the last disclosing seven more. In addition to this structure there is a parenthesis between the sixth and the seventh in all three series.[20]

The idea here is that the silence needs to be understood in light of Revelation 6:12 through Revelation 19:14 which states that at the beginning and consummation of the judgment the rider, whose name is Faithful and True, and the Word of God, will come on a white horse with the armies of heaven. In regards to the judgment at the consummation there is the argument that the heavenly host will empty the celestial courts to accompany Christ

---

[19] Cf. Bernard P. Dausenhauer (1980), Silence: The Phenomenon and its Significance (Bloomington: Indiana University Press), 10-15.
[20] David Grey Barnhouse (1971), Revelation an Expository Commentary (Grand Rapids, Michigan: Zondervan), 155.

to earth (cf. Rev 1:7; Matt 25:31).[21] The silence is a silence of awesome expectation of the things that are about to occur. The wrath of God is to be poured out on the disobedient. The silence thus forms a bridge between the opening of the seals and these great events. With the seventh seal the revelation is not complete, for there is still more to be explained concerning God's program of events in the great controversy with evil.[22] George Eldon Ladd says that the silence is an attitude of trembling suspense by the heavenly hosts in view of the judgments of God, which are about to fall upon the world. "It is the silence of dreadful anticipation of the events that are about to ensue, now that the time of the end has come".[23]

Fig: 1:1

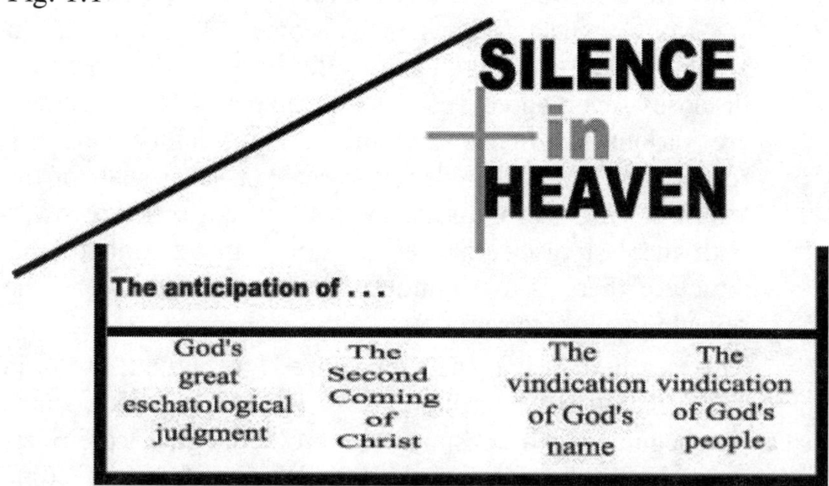

Varlene Youngberg, who proposes that there was silence in heaven when Jesus in his priestly passion took on the sins of the

[21] F. D. Nichol, general editor, (1980 printing) The Seventh-day Adventist Bible Commentary, volume 10 (Washington, D, C.: Review and Herald), 266, 267.

[22] Ibid.

[23] George Eldon Ladd (1972), A Commentary on the Revelation of John (Grand Rapids, MI.: Wm. B. Eerdmans), 123.

world and prayed in the garden of Gethsemane, has offered an interesting view. He says, that at the end of the heavenly court judgment scene, which is recorded in Revelation 4, 5 (cf. Daniel 7:9-14), Jesus carries away the sins confessed by the saints. The idea is that "As the seventh seal opens in the heavenly sanctuary, the angels again lay down their harps. Silence reigns for Jesus again takes sin on His body."[24] Of interest here is the "holy silence" which some scholars have argued was associated with the sacrifice of the ancient Hebrew temple. The inner circle of the sanctuary was that of the priest, in which the sacred service was offered in absolute silence, while in contrast, the outer circle was that of folk prayers; the central circle was the place where the Levites sang. As the priests offered sacrifice in the inner sanctum all was silent throughout the circles. The silence was so complete that often it was felt no person was present. On the Day of Atonement the trumpet was blown to gather the people and announce the solemnity of worship. After the people gathered and the priest went into the inner sanctum, silence was practiced until he returned to the altar in the front of the court. A prayer was offered in the temple, but not in the holy of holies, nor was it offered with the offering or with the sprinkling of blood. It was offered in the outer court before the sacrifice began. It is not clear whether this dynamic between sound and silence was as distinct in the second temple, but a note from Alfred Edersheim states that as the temple president gave the command that it was time for the incense to begin, the whole multitude withdrew from the inner court and fell down before the Lord, spreading their hands in silent prayer. Then throughout the temple building deep silence rested on the multitude as the priest offering the sacrifice bowed down or prayed while withdrawing backwards from the Holy Place (cf. Lev 16:17; 1 Chron 16; 2 Chron 29:20-36; Num

---

[24] Varlene Youngberg (1977), The Revelation of Jesus Christ to His People (Keene, TX, Southern Color Graphics), 211.

10:10).[25] The evidence is that although many features of the silence persisted in the second temple as time progressed, much of the original silence was destroyed with the original structure. But the point remains that there seems to have been some understanding that at the moment when the divine pronounced judgment there was necessary silence in the temple.[26]

Judgment takes place from the celestial sphere, but since the correspondence between the celestial and the terrestrial spheres carried a great significance in Jewish understanding, the observation was that when God broke into the terrestrial sphere there was need for silence. The persistent view was that heaven is God's sanctuary and the seat of His rule (1 Kings 22:19-22; Isa 6:1ff; Job 1:6ff; Dan 7:9ff), it is the point from which He brings His manifestation to the world. It is the sphere from which He controls the destinies of empires and the lives of individual human beings (Dan 2:18ff. 28, 37, 44; Ezr 5:11f.; 6:9f.; 7:12, 23). It is therefore the point from which the rhythm of sound and silence comes.

A most interesting view of the reason for the silence, which is to the right of the general spectrum of views, maintains that the heavenly silence signifies "the millennial rest of the Church" following on the final conclusion and resolution designated by the earthquake and the preceding sixth seal.[27] Diametric to this view is the notion that the silence is a simple rhetorical style for the organization of John's series of sevens such as his seven seals, seven trumpets and seven vials.[28] This view is not popular but very appealing to critical scholars who

---

[25] Alfred Edershein (1919), The Temple: Its Ministry and Services: As They Were at the Time of Jesus Christ (Grand Rapids, MI: Wm. B. Eerdmans), 167.

[26] See Israel Knohl, "Between Voice and Silence: The Relationship Between Prayer and the Temple Cult," Journal of Biblical Literature 115:1 (1996), 17-30 for a good review of the issues involved.

[27] E. B. Elliot (1862), A Commentary on the Apocalypse Vol. 1 (London: John Childs and Sons), 322.

[28] Ibid, 323.

argue that the pause simply follows the prophetic strategy that uses the pause to signal a solemn event such as the day of Yahweh.[29] A view that is not often discussed is that from the prophetic/apocalyptic nature of Revelation we need to see that the half an hour is a time line based on Ezekiel 14: 6 and Numbers 14:34, which makes the *half an hour* equivalent to seven days or a week. The idea is that if in prophetic symbolism "a day is equivalent to a year," then half an hour is equal to seven days. Within the seven days Jesus will come to earth and return to heaven. This will allow for a seventh day celebration on the Sea of Glass.[30]

Many of the views are fascinating and point us to something of profound significance; namely, that silence is multifaceted and mysterious and cannot be easily deciphered. Arnaldo Nesti says that silence has the potential to invade and permeate a social space; it is a resource capable of moving the deepest hidden roots. Among the multiple forms of silence Nesti notes, there is a closing silence, a reservedness of mortified silence, a menacing silence, an angry silence and a sullen silence, a silence that carries a load of memories without recalling one in particular, a silence that considers all the options without choosing any. There is the admiring silence and the contemptuous silence. There is a silence that can rise from indifference and one that issues from bias. Silence might mean a refusal to communicate with another being, or, which is even more serious the incapacity to do so. It is not always the silence of the mouth that allows a deeper communication than that of words. There is a silence of the soul that sometimes hides itself under a flow of words. At its ultimate, silence is used

---

[29] Cf. Raymond E. Brown, et al. (1968), The Jerome Biblical Commentary (Englewood Cliffs, N. J.: Prentice Hall), 477, 478.

[30] This is one of the least popular views among Christians, but has a very interesting perspective for those who carry a radical prophetic apocalyptic interpretation of Revelation.

predominantly in metaphoric ways to express experiences on the boundaries of human communication.[31]

But all of the above explanations still leave us with the question, "What does it mean that God is silent?" For in our human frame this is still a profound and enigmatic thing. What we can know is that the divine silence has theological, theodicical, psychological, and philosophical significance. It is very well linked to the existential experience of the human connection with the divine. When the prophet Habakkuk confronted a moment of heavenly silence, he cried out: "How long O Lord, must I call for help, but you do not listen? Or cry out to you, 'Violence!' but you do not save? Why do you make me look at injustice? Why do you tolerate wrong? Destruction and violence are before me; there is strife, and conflict abounds. Therefore the law is paralyzed, and justice never prevails. The wicked hem in righteousness, so that justice is perverted" (Hab 1:2-4). David cried, "To you, O Lord, I call; my rock, do not refuse to hear me, for if you are silent to me, I shall be like those who go down to the Pit" (Psa 28:1). "Do not be silent, O God of my praise" (Psa 109:1). Asaph said, "O God, do not keep silence; do not hold your peace or be still, O God!" (Psa 83:1). While Isaiah asked, "After all this, will you restrain yourself, O Lord? Will you keep silent, and punish us so severely?" (Isa 64:12).

The heavenly silence and the faith experience of the people of God.

My interest here is not just to interpret a text but also to see what message the silence in the text bears for the faith experience of those who are awaiting the Second Coming of Christ. Too often in awaiting the coming of Christ we want to hear and know everything, because we cannot deal with the divine

[31] Arnaldo Nesti, "Silence as Elsewhere," Social Compass 42:4 (1995), 421-431.

silence concerning the day or date of it. Especially since we are confronting the beginning of another millennium, there is grave concern about unraveling this mystery of history. We want to know when history will conclude and how the kingdom of God will be established, but there is silence. What will happen to the saints if they cannot hear God's voice for half an hour? Do we prefer being confronted by a God who is speaking (revealing himself) or by one who is silent (hiding himself)? What happens when there seems to be a loss of the intimate presence? Though the servants of God are evidently told what is to take place in the consummation (Dan 12:1ff; Rev 4:1; 22:6), not everything is told (Dan 12:9; Rev 22:10). The author of Revelation point to the need for silence in two of his other epistles that bear his given name in the following way:

> I have much to write to you, but I do not want to use paper and ink. Instead, I hope to visit you and talk to you face to face, so that our joy may be complete (2 Jn 12).

> I have much to write to you, but I do not want to do so with pen and ink. Instead, I hope to see you soon and we will talk face to face. (3 Jn 13, 14).

My total interest in this study thus focuses upon the challenge of these silences. Based upon the reality that heaven seems to be a place of constant sounds, there is need to ask, Can heaven be contemplated as a place of silence, solitude and rest? Since we are constantly bombarded by sounds in our everyday world,[32] there is a basis for our interest in a voiceless heaven. "What happens when Jesus stops responding to the prayers of the saints?" What will happen when probation closes? What happens when we face oppression, injustice and persecution, and we want

[32] Margaret Guenther, "Embracing the Silence," Christian Century 12:19 (June 7, 1995), 603.

a heaven that is responsive with speech, power, judgment, comfort and dialogue--not silence, and there is none? How can God be silent in our suffering? How can we embrace a God that is silent?

Among Christians there is the awareness that Jesus Christ promised that He would return (Jn 14:1-3). There is the awareness that at His coming He will be escorted by a host of angels (Rev 19:11-19; cf. Matt 25:31). Does this truly mean that heaven will be emptied of all its occupants? The challenges of God's silence are often grievous to us. Is there a reason behind God's silence? What shall we do when God refuses to give Himself to us? What shall we suspect when there is no voice -- no praise -- no hallelujahs, no thunder and no quake? Again, is God hiding from us? Will God turn away from us? Are we confronting the *Deus abscunditus*? The consequences of silence can be negative anxiety as well as positive anxiety. From the negative side we think of silence as a confrontation with suffering, hopelessness, destruction, agony and anonymity, and judgment. From the positive side we see faith, hope, and the mystical life that leads beyond death to the vindication of God. Here we can contemplate silence. To build the positive perspective, I have taken the liberty of decontextualizing a text in Job to make it a prayer to God. These are words said by Job to Eliphaz, his mocking friend: "Teach me and I shall be silent, make me understand how I have gone wrong." (Job 6:24).

The point I am seeking to make is that God can speak for Himself. Isaiah says, "For Zion's sake I will not keep silent, and for Jerusalem's sake I will not rest, until her vindication shines out like the dawn, and her salvation like a burning torch" (Isa 62:1). "See, it is written before me; I will not keep silent, but I will repay; I will indeed repay in their laps"(Isa 65: 6). At other times God chooses to be silent. The same Isaiah says, "He was oppressed, and he was afflicted, yet he did not open his mouth; like a Lamb that is led to the slaughter, and like a sheep that is before its sharers is silent, so he did not open his mouth" (Isa 53:

7). "Have I not kept silent and closed my eyes, and so you do not fear me" (Isa 57: 11). "After all this, will you restrain yourself, O Lord? Will you keep silent, and punish us so severely?" (Isa 64: 12). It is from such a perspective that I examine "silence in heaven."

Some methodological issues in understanding the heavenly silence

My methodology in this investigation is to be biblical, theological, philosophical and psychological. The biblical and theological interest focuses on Revelation 8:1, as it appears in its own and in the broader biblical context. The biblical hermeneutical principle is fundamental to the best traditions of Scriptural interpretation.[33] It takes into account the polarity of the paradigm, which is basic to the apocalyptic understanding of history as it appears in Revelation. A majority of scholars have argued that the great themes of Revelation, such as its central theme of God as the ruler of the universe, ruling from His celestial sphere, followed by the themes of worship and judgment and the manifestation of Christ as the "One who is, who was, and who is coming" are all structured in an apocalyptic and prophetic manner. A. H. Abrams says that apocalyptic narrative and prophecy is a *chiaroscuro* history, that is a history in which there are opponent forces of light and darkness. Therefore, there is no middle ground between the totally good and the absolutely evil. On the negative side are arraigned Satan, the beast, the great whore "Babylon the Great, the Mother of Harlots and Abominations of the Earth," together with the earthly agents of iniquity ("the kings of the earth" and their armies) to whom

---

[33] Kenneth Strand (1992),"Foundational Principles of Interpretation" in Symposium on Revelation, Book II (Frank Holbrook, ed., Silver Spring, MD: Biblical Research Institute, General Conference of Seventh-day Adventists).

exegetes have applied the term "Antichrist." Opposed to them are God, Christ, and the New Jerusalem "which is prepared as a bride adorned for her husband"(Rev 21: 2), along with the company of earthly saints. From the apocalyptic perspective, the consummation of history will occur not by mediation between the polar opposites, but only after the extirpation of the forces of evil by the forces of good.[34] At such a time God need not say a word, though He does.

In addition to Abrams' point, we can note the Scriptural and historical perspective that whenever the people of God confront suffering, or profound theological and theodicical questions, they generally turn to apocalyptic. I use a figure to illustrate the poles accented in apocalyptic and prophetic speech.

Fig 1:2

The intervention of God	**The present crisis**
Focus on the certain future life	Focus on the uncertain present life
The forces of light (good)	The forces of darkness (iniquity)
Manifestation of the power of God	Manifestation of the power of evil
The coming of Christ	The coming of the Antichrist
The judgment of the righteous	The judgment of the wicked
Resurrection to life	Destruction of the world by fire, flood, astronomical catastrophe, etc.
Salvation of the righteous	Destruction of the wicked

[34] M. H. Abrams (1988), "Apocalypse: Theme and Romantic Variations," in The Revelation of St. John the Divine, (edited by Harold Bloom, New York: Chelsea House), 11.

Eternal life (Heaven)	Eternal death (Hell)
Peace and eternal rest	The eternal struggle

Most of the messages of Revelation are steeped in the above poles of apocalyptic symbolisms. Sometimes the symbolisms are vague, but no one can say that they have not always tended to arouse deep thoughts and feelings. My own conviction is that one cannot study Revelation 8:1 without bringing forward such thoughts and feelings. And such subjective and objective thoughts and emotions are not always negative, for the intent of the book is to challenge the people of God to faithfulness despite the pressure and persecution that they face. Whatever circumstances may be, the prophet wants us to know that God is faithful to lead us to victory (Rev 1:7, 8; 11:15-19; cf. 22:12-13).

A practical point to remember about the book of Revelation, such as is true of all other biblical books is that the author did not sit down and develop a certain method, as we speak of interpretive methods today. Rather, from his own contextual and existential situation he wrote his work. In the case of Revelation, the author wrote to persecuted Christians under the Roman state who needed reassurance that the divine Christ was present with his people even in their day (Rev 1:17, 18). He therefore chose material and methods that suited the particular situation with which he needed to deal. On the whole, he focuses on cosmic, earthly historical and personal realities. He also shows that the God who rules the world is in a position of transcendence. God's throne, God's temple is in heaven. In spite of His silence God is not under the control of any mortal. John uses his codes and organizes his content and presents his structure with multiple referent points to point to the fact that God's ways are past finding out. In the mystery of the apocalyptic and prophetic we can find the God of silence.

Our limitations in understanding the heavenly silence

Much about the "half an hour" of silence in heaven remains a mystery and this study cannot pretend to resolve the incomprehensibility of all the sounds of silence. For example, in our understanding of time we speak of eternity, millennia, centuries, years, months, weeks, days, hours, minutes, seconds, nanoseconds and so on. But we do not understand all of these dimensions. And none give us a complete orientation to heavenly time. However, I attempt to work through the many ambiguities that are notable to focus on that which goes before and that which arises from the time of heavenly silence. In this vein, I cover the specific themes of heaven as a place of sound and silence, what it means when God is silent, silence and the judgment of God, silence and the Second Coming of Christ, and why the people of God can embrace the heavenly silence.

Appropriating three significant themes encircling Revelation 8:1

The above themes make the interpretation of Revelation interesting. However, since in the total context of Revelation 8:1 one finds three persistent ideas, we give them passing attention as we set the stage for the larger discussion.

Silence and the heavenly temple scene

The first idea has to do with John's great emphasis on the heavenly temple or sanctuary (*naos cf. Rev 4; 5; 7; 8; 10; 11; 14; 21-22*), which is quite unique among the authors of the Old and New Testament. While the other biblical authors speak to the issue of heaven or the heavenly temple, not all linger on it, as does John. For John, the cosmic and transcendent reality is the total focus of history. Even Ezekiel from whom John draws much of his imagery pays more attention to the earthly Jerusalem rather than the heavenly. In the New Testament Matthew pays much attention to heavenly realities but he treats them in light of earthly realities. Matthew uses the word "heaven" in reference to the kingdom of God. But Matthew does not focus on the transcendent temple imagery as John does. John keeps the mind focused upward. And from the moment he introduces us to the heavenly realities in the scenes of worship around the throne (Rev 4, 5), he does not pause until he brings heaven to earth as "the holy city," "the New Jerusalem" which "comes down from God out of heaven" (Rev 21:10). When one considers the other words and phrases that John uses for heaven, one can argue that, of all biblical authors, he gives the greatest attention to the subject. And what is presented is, as Jacques Ellul says it, not a falsehood, but a sign, not a material reality, but truth, not legend, but the revealed word, not a description, but a message, not identity, but identification. That is to say the reality of heaven is much beyond that which any human pen, even under inspiration, can describe. But what is presented is offered so that humanity can know what God's final intention is for those who love Him.[35]

For the biblical ancients, the tent or tabernacle (*skene*), which became the temple or sanctuary (*naos*) was God's dwelling place. They spoke of it as the seat of His rule. Thus when God was pleased with His people He came to the tent, tabernacle, temple or sanctuary. When His people were disobedient, He left to some "hinterland"[36] as an action of judgment and rebuke. John uses the imagery of the earthly tent, tabernacle, temple, sanctuary, but he transposes them to the heavenly temple.[37] His interest is wholly cosmic, and the earthly temple/sanctuary has been

---

[35] Jacques Ellul (1970), The Meaning of the City (Grand Rapids, MI.: Wm. B. Eerdmans), 173.

[36] See R. Dean Davis (1992), The Heavenly Court Judgment of Revelation 4-5 (Latham, MD: University Press of America,), 20-21, for a more extensive discussion of the concept of God dwelling in the earthly tabernacle, temple, and sanctuary.

[37] Cf. Ibid.

destroyed (ACE 70). C. Mervyn Maxwell and a host of other scholars have noted that the heavenly sanctuary is a central pivot in the message of Revelation and that five of the numbers of major divisions of the book are introduced with scenes that center on it.[38]

My conclusion is that to understand the language of "the tabernacle," "the temple," "the sanctuary," "the throne," as referenced by John, one must turn every thought heavenward. Here one is to note that John understood the affirmation of faith that if God is in heaven all will be well on earth.[39] Jesus made the same point in the opening phrase of the model prayer. "Our Father in heaven, hallowed is your name. Your Kingdom come. Your will be done, on earth, as it is in heaven" (Matt 6:9, 10). For the author of the Hebrews there is a contrast between the priestly ministry of Christ in the heavens and that of the earthly priests. "Christ," he says, "did not enter a sanctuary made by human hands, a mere copy of the true one, but he entered *into heaven itself*, now to appear in the presence of God for us" (Heb 9:24, Italics supplied). When John concludes the Revelation, he says that the home of God is with mortals. God will dwell with them and they shall be His people. God Himself will be with them (Rev 21:3). Here the point of interest is that in the New Jerusalem there will be no temple (Rev 21:22), for the Lord God is its

---

[38] C. Mervyn Maxwell (1985), God Cares: The Message of Revelation For You and Your Family (Boise, Idaho: Pacific Press Publishing Association), 164, 165. He outlines the scenes of the seven churches, the seven seals, the seven trumpets, the great controversy and the seven last plagues, all taking place from the sanctuary. Kenneth Strand (1992),"Foundational Principles of Interpretation" in Symposium on Revelation, Book II (Frank Holbrook, ed., Silver Spring, MD: Biblical Research Institute, General Conference of Seventh-day Adventists).

[39] cf. Renita J. Weems (1999). Listening for God: A Minister's Journey Through Silence and Doubt (New York: Simon & Schuster). She suggests that in as much as we affirm this, there is still mystery that confronts each of us when God does not seem to answer us sometimes.

temple. It is very likely that, for John, all of heaven is the temple, for it is the most transparent place of the divine revelation.[40] We conclude then that John's focus is not so much on a physical structure called a tent, tabernacle, temple or sanctuary building, as it is on the reality that God is judge in His house.

Silence and the eschatological judgment of God

A clear connection is set between the temple, silence and the judgment of God. While in Revelation 8:1 John does not so much as use any word for *judgment*, his whole context is that of judgment. The whole book is, in fact, a book about judgment. The messages to the seven churches specify judgment. The last of the seven churches is referenced as *Laodicia*, "a people adjudged." The story of the inaugurated Christ is set in judgment (Rev 4-5). The picture of the seven seals is set in judgment (Rev 6, 7). The silence of Revelation 8:1 brings the interchange between the focus of judgment on the church and the judgment on the world. When John pushes forward from Revelation 8:2 he focuses on the judgment of the wicked and the vindication of the people of God. After the half an hour of silence the trumpets introduce the new stage of judgment.

We have noted that trumpets were used in ancient times to call attention to Israel's sacred days. In Israel the trumpet was the instrument of choice for calling the people of God to the great festival days and to the most solemn of all days, the Day of Atonement (cf. Num 10:1ff).[41] It is most appropriate here,

---

[40] Leon Morris (1987), Revelation: Tyndale New Testament Commentaries, (Grand Rapids: MI.: Wm. B. Eerdmans), 115.
[41] cf. R. Dean Davis (1992), The Heavenly Court Judgment of Revelation 4-5 (Latham, MD: University Press of America), for a larger discussion of the use of the trumpet as an instrument of proclamation.

therefore, to pay attention to the silence that calls the universe to the most solemn time of God's judgment.

When John points to the activity in heaven, he notes that heaven is not just a worship room, but also a courtroom (Rev 4,5 cf. Dan 7:26). The facts that we have recited are that each of the seven seals brings an action of judgment upon the people of God (Rev 6-8). The next scenes of the judgment are those announced in the seven trumpets, which bring judgment upon the world (Rev 9-11). In the battle with the dragon, the beast(s), and the false powers, there is judgment (Rev 12-14). In the great proclamation of God's final message to humankind, the overarching theme is judgment (Rev 14: 6-12). In the outpouring of the plagues there is judgment (Rev 15-16). The fall of Babylon is a decisive action of judgment (Rev 17-19). In the consummation of history there is judgment (Rev 20:1-22).

In effect, judgment is the rule of God's throne. God is judge. His judgment involves all human beings; it involves the Church and the world. It involves all the powers of evil. It speaks to temporal judgment and the eternal judgment. It speaks to the judgment as inaugurated and the judgment as it is to be consummated. The character of the judge is what brings judgment. At the Second Coming the judgment is consummated (Rev 20:7-22).

Silence and the Second Coming of Christ

The Second Coming of Christ is not named in Revelation 8:1, but is the total context from which it is drawn and to which it projects. Any cursory reading of its "preface" in Revelation 6:12-7:17, which marks the opening of the sixth seal, through which the whole universe is shattered, the end time trouble is experienced, and the rescue and reward of the saints is secured, cannot fail to identify the Second Coming as the great event to which all of history's silence is oriented. Christ, the Lamb of God, who opens the seventh seal (8:1 f. p.), is the One who is to come with clouds and whom every eye will see (Rev 1:7). He is the One who will come quickly (3:11; 22:7). He is seen as a man on "a white horse," leading "the armies of heaven." With His "sword in His hand," and His "robe dipped in blood," and His crown (diadem) on His head, and the title "King of kings and Lord of lords" on His vesture, He will come (c.f. 19). He is the one who will speak in the trumpet voice so that the dead in Christ shall rise first (1 Thess 4:14). He is the One who will cause the wicked to call to the mountains and rocks, saying, "Fall on us and hide us from the face of the one seated on the throne and from the wrath of the Lamb!" (Rev 6:16). He comes out of silence and speaks His word of judgment.

We noted earlier that among the multiple interpretations concerning the half an hour of silence, one persistent interpretation is that heaven will be emptied of all the hosts who will accompany Christ at His appearing.[42] We think it proper also to add that the Second Coming may not only lead to "a silent heaven" but also "a silent earth." At least, this is the picture that I have extracted from the Old Testament prophets (cf. 1 Sam 2:9; Jer 48:9; 49:2; 50:13; Isa 13:9; 15:1; 41:1; Ez 6:14; 30:7) and also from the *Apocalypse* (cf. Rev 19, and 20 on the images of desolation). These realities of silence, in the face of the contrasting sounds of heaven and earth, are the reasons for this study. To experience the silence of heaven, the Second Coming of Christ and the earth at rest, and heaven at last, not only opens up new spaces for sounds but also more time for the realities of silence. Let us study Revelation 8:1 further and listen to the sounds of silence, for already in the silence we can anticipate the climatic culmination of history. In it we anticipate God's eternal Sabbath rest. We also anticipate the vindication of God and God's people, and God's final word.

---

[42] F. D. Nichol, general editor, (1980 printing), The Seventh-day Adventist Bible Commentary, vol. 10, (Washington, D, C.: Review and Herald), 787.

“There was silence in heaven for the space of half and hour” (Revelation 8:1).

“On that day I will answer, says the Lord, I will answer the heavens and they shall answer the earth . . .” (Hosea 2:21).

II

BETWEEN SOUND AND SILENCE: HEAVEN IS A PLACE OF SOUNDS AND SILENCE

Between sound and silence

Just as the presence of sound communicates information to us, so does the absence of sound. One has to be always struck by the dialectical interplay between both.[43] Bernard Dauenhauer says, "without utterance there can be no silence," for silence never ceases to imply its opposite and to depend on its presence.[44] The phrase "There was silence in heaven about the space of half an hour," in Revelation 8:1, leads us to contemplate the most dramatic accentuations of heavenly sound and silence that can be found in any one book of Scripture. While the rest of Scripture gives great emphasis to the sounds of earth in uplifted worship to God, Revelation puts the emphasis on sound and silence, mainly from heaven. The book begins when the Divine first calls the attention of John to the messages to be given to His Church concerning the things that must shortly come to pass (Rev 1:19; 4:1) including the Second Coming (1:7,8). The conclusion of the book is thus reached when the same voice states, "Yes, I am coming soon" (22:20).

---

[43] Robert G. King (1979), Fundamentals of Human Communication (New York: Macmillan), 261.

[44] Bernard P. Dausenhauer (1980) Silence: The Phenomenon and its Significance (Bloomington, Indiana: University Press), 5.

Throughout the book there is a constant appeal to "see," and "hear" (1:3; 2:7, 11, 17, 29; 3:6,13, 22) what is being said in addition to what one might suspect has not been said.

To understand what is taking place in the dynamics of sound and silence encircling Revelation 8:1, one must understand the immediate context of the text as well as its broader context which harkens both back to the first chapter where the Almighty speaks from heaven, and to the conclusion of the book, where He speaks His last word. It is quite unsettling to think of this last word, and to find a passage such as Revelation 8:1 sitting in the midst of all of the zestful sounds. It pushes one to ask, "What is this silence? What can it mean? But let us suspend the questions a little while, for one can only understand the silence as one understands the sounds. The point that has been made about Revelation is that it is a book of sights and sounds.

Majestic sounds

The picture of heaven, which John mostly presents, is that it is a place of sounds. We have noted already that the book begins with the sound of the divine voice, which sounds like a trumpet in Revelation 1:10. But it is in the fourth and fifth chapters --what most commentators would call the frontal outer limit of 8:1-- that we hear a crescendo of worshipful sounds. In these chapters is the description of a majestic worship celebration in the sanctuary of heaven. The scene is the inauguration or enthronement of Christ as Lord, who took His seat at the side of God, as Karl Barth says, "in direct fellowship with Him, in full participation of His glory."[45] John's portrayal begins with a picture of God through the "open door" in heaven (Rev 4:1). For a second time John hears a voice like a trumpet. As he turns to look and listen more carefully, he sees God sitting upon a throne, surrounded by twenty-four elders.

---

[45] Karl Barth (Latest impression 1989), Church Dogmatics: IV: 2: The Doctrine of Reconciliation (Edinburgh: T&T Clark), 153.

From the throne come "lightning" and "thundering." In the center, around the throne, are also four living creatures covered with eyes in the front and on their backs. "Day and night they never stop saying, 'Holy, holy, holy is the Lord God Almighty, who was, and is, and is to come'" (Rev 4:8). Whenever the living creatures give glory, honor and thanks to God who sits on the throne and lives forever and ever, the twenty-four elders fall down before God who sits on the throne and worship Him. They lay their crowns before the throne and say, "You are worthy, our Lord and God, to receive glory and honor and power, for you created all things, and by your will they were created and have their being" (Rev 4:11).

God is given worshipful praise because He is Creator and Sustainer. He is worshipped, not just because of what He does but also because of who He is. He is Sovereign. He rules the world. He is above all creatures and potentates. He is worthy to receive glory and honor and praise.

In the midst of the worship, a crisis seems to develop, and there is an evident pause while a question is raised. The question is generated because in the hand of the one seated on the throne there is a scroll, sealed with seven seals on both sides, and someone is needed to open the seals. Good reflection might lead to the memory that in the book of Daniel understanding concerning the divine words was sealed until the time of the end (Daniel 12:9). As the time of the end approaches, a mighty angel therefore asks in a loud tone, "Who is ready to open the scroll or even look inside of it?" The response is offered that no one is worthy to open the scroll except the Lion of the tribe of Judah, for He has been slain and has given His life for the world. When He takes the scroll from the One on the throne, the twenty-four elders and all the occupants of heaven begin to play their harps and sing a new song:

"You are worthy to take the scroll and to open its seals, because you were slain, and with your blood you purchased men for God from every tribe and language and people and nation. You have them to be a kingdom and priests to serve our God, and they will reign on the earth" (Rev 5:9, 10).

The worship is heightened when John hears the voices of many thousands and thousands of angels who are encircling the throne along with the twenty-four elders. In a louder voice they sing (5:11):

> "Worthy is the Lamb who was slain, to receive power and wealth and wisdom and strength and honor and glory and praise" (Rev 5:12).

Then all the creatures in heaven and earth and under the earth and in the sea sing:

> "To him who sits on the throne and to the Lamb are praise and honor and glory and power, forever and ever!" (5:13)

The four living creatures then say "Amen," and the elders fall down and worship (5:14). The worship in chapter four focuses on the Creator, and in the fifth chapter on the Lamb and the victory on the cross. Jon Paulien has put it nicely when he says that:

> There is deliberate progression of thought in the five hymns of this introductory scene. Two hymns are addressed to the Father (4:8, 11). The next two are addressed to the Lamb (5:9-10, 11-12). The fifth and final hymn is addressed to both the Father and the Lamb (5:13).

That the equality of praise is the explicit highlight of the backdrop is evident from the ever-increasing volume of participants . . . . This ever-increasing participation indicates that it is heaven's greatest joy to exalt Jesus Christ even as His Father is exalted (cf. John 5:23).

The all-encompassing language of 5:13 suggests that this hymn is proleptic (portrayed in advance) of the entire universe in praise to God (cf. Phil 2:9-11). Therefore while the scene of chapter 5 highlights the enthronement of Christ at the beginning of the age, it also points forward to the universal rejoicing at the end.[46]

The above is just the beginning of the heavenly praises and noises that have laced the book of Revelation. As the seven seals are being opened there is the further progress of heavenly sounds. With the opening of the first of the seven seals one of the four living creatures invites John in a "thunderous" voice to come! And look at the first scene in the drama. When the second seal is opened, a second living creature, again, invites John to come! The same is repeated in the opening of the third and fourth seals. In the opening of the fifth seal the voices of the saints "under the altar" are heard. So as not to digress, I join other commentators in stating that no effort is being made to explain the state of the dead[47] or to show that there are singing saints up in heaven now. The point is that God is always willing to hear the prayers of his people. No matter how long His answer is in coming, their cries are ever present to Him.

As the scene shifts to the earth with the opening of the sixth seal, the sound of an earthquake is heard (6:1-16). The sound on the earth is very connected with heaven, for the activities in heaven impact the earth (cf. Rev 6:13; Matt 6:10). With the opening of the sixth seal there seems to be a pause in the order of the action as an angel coming from the east calls out in a loud voice to the four angels that were given power to harm the earth. He tells them not to hurt the land, nor the sea or any trees until the servants of God are sealed in their foreheads (cf. 7:1-3). In effect, up to this point there is no pause in the voices and liturgical sounds, but there are pauses in the action.

To experience the silence of Revelation 8:1 is therefore profound and challenging. But let us quickly move beyond the

---

[46] Jon. Paulien (1992), "The Seven Seals," in Symposium on Revelation, Book I, edited by Frank Holbrook (Silver Spring, MD: Biblical Research Institute), 207.

[47] Ibid., 235.

silence; for following the silence there are seven trumpets. The first five trumpets sound and many activities take place on the earth. Then the sixth trumpet sounds and again noise is heard from the horns of the golden altar that is before God. Of significance is the fact that whereas in the fifth seal the focus of the sound was moved to the earth, now in the sixth trumpet the focus of the sound returns to heaven (Rev 8, 9).

Again there seems to be a pause and change in action when in the scene of Revelation 10 an angel comes from heaven with a little scroll. John hears another angel from heaven commanding him in a loud voice to take the scroll and eat it. It would be sweet in John's mouth and bitter in his stomach (Rev 10).

At the sounding of the seventh trumpet there are loud voices in heaven saying:

> "The kingdom of this world has become the kingdom of our Lord and of his Christ, and he will reign forever and ever" (11:15).

Then the twenty-four elders who were seated near the throne, already spoken of in the fourth and fifth chapters, come forth saying in a loud voice:

> "We give thanks to you, Lord God Almighty, the One who is and who was, because you have taken your great power and have begun to reign. The nations were angry; and your wrath has come. The time has come for judging the dead, and for rewarding your servants the prophets and your saints and those who reverence your name, both small and great -- and for destroying those who destroy the earth" (11:17-18).

Then the temple of God opens in heaven and the Ark of the Covenant is seen. John sees flashes of lightning, and hears rumbling, peals of thunder and an earthquake and great hailstorms (11:18).

When Michael gains the victory over the dragon in the great cosmic conflict, a loud voice is heard in heaven saying:

> "Now is come salvation and the power and the kingdom of our God, and the authority of his Christ. For the accuser of our brothers, who accuses them before God day and night, has been hurled down. They overcome him by the blood of the Lamb and the word of their testimony; they did not love their lives so much as to shrink from death. Therefore rejoice you heavens and you who dwell in them! But woe to the earth and the sea, because the devil has gone down to you! He is filled with fury, because he knows that his time is short" (12:10-12).

In his description of the victorious saints who stand on Mount Zion, John hears a tumultuous voice from heaven like the sound of many rushing waters and like a loud peal of thunder. The sound is like harpists playing their harps. They sing a new song before the throne and before the four living creatures and the elders. No one can learn the song except the 144,000 who have been redeemed from the earth. (14:1-5). Following the third of the three angels' messages, there is heard another voice from heaven saying: "Write; Blessed are the dead who die in the Lord from now on." "Yes, says the Spirit, they will rest from their labor for their deeds will follow them" (14:13).

When the harvest of the earth is reaped, the angel coming from the heavenly altar calls in a loud voice to the angel coming out of the temple of God, saying "Take your sharp sickle and gather the clusters of the earth's vine, because its grapes are ripe" (14:14-18). Contrasted with the scene of the angels and the seven last plagues is the scene of those who have been victorious over the beast. As they stand on the sea, "They held harps given to them by God and sang the song of Moses the servant of God and the song of the Lamb" (15:1,2), saying:

> "Great and marvelous are your deeds, Lord God Almighty. Just and true are your ways, King of the ages. Who will not fear you, O Lord, and bring glory to your name? For you alone are holy. All nations will come and worship

> before you, for your righteous acts have been revealed" (15:3, 4).

From the heavenly temple a loud voice tells the angels with the seven last plagues to go pour out the bowls of God's wrath on the earth. In response to the action of the third angel, who pours out his bowl on the sea, the angel who has charge of the waters shouts:

> "You are just in your judgments, you who are and who were, the Holy One, because you have so judged; for they have shed the blood of your saints and the prophets, and you have given them blood to drink as they deserve" (16:5, 6).

Even the heavenly altar responds: "Yes, Lord God Almighty, true and just are your judgments" (16:7).

When the seventh angel pours out his bowl into the air, again, a loud voice comes out of the heavenly temple saying; "It is done." Flashes of lightning, rumbling, peals of thunder and an earthquake follow this (16:17, 18). Again, though some of the sounds seem to be more earthly than heavenly, they are closely related and cannot be disconnected. The sounds from the heavenly temple are heard on earth. Of interest is the fact that an angel with a "mighty voice announces from heaven the fall of Babylon which is heard on earth (18:2, 3). Another angelic voice from heaven calls forth the true believers from Babylon:

> "Come out of her, my people, so that you will not share in her sins, so that you will not receive her plagues; for her sins are piled up to heaven, and God has remembered her crimes. Give back to her as she has given; pay her back double for what she has done. Mix her a double portion from her own cup. Give her as much torture and grief as the glory she gave herself." In her heart she boasts, "I sit a queen, I am not a widow, and I will never mourn." Therefore in one day her plagues will overtake her: death,

> mourning and famine. She will be consumed by fire, for mighty is the Lord God who judges her" (18:4-8).

In the celebration of the marriage of the Bride and the Lamb, the heavenly sounds are heightened, for they signal the last word of the redeemed against the dragon, the beast and the false prophet and their first great heavenly word to the Lamb. They are ecstatic, to state it mildly. They shout their words in a majestic *Hallel*:

> "Hallelujah! Salvation and glory and power belong to God, for true and just are your judgments. He has condemned the great prostitute who corrupted the earth by her adulteries. He has avenged on her the blood of his servants." And again they shouted: "Hallelujah! The smoke from her goes up for ever and ever." The twenty-four elders and the four living creatures fell down and worshipped God who was seated on the throne. And they cried. "Amen, Hallelujah!" Then a voice came from the one saying: "Praise our God, all you his servants, you who fear him, both small and great!" Then I heard what sounded like a great multitude, like the roar of rushing waters and like loud peals of thunder, shouting: "Hallelujah! For our Lord God Almighty reigns. Let us rejoice and be glad and give him glory! For the wedding of the lamb has come and his bride has made herself ready. Fine linen, bright and clean, was given to her to wear" (19:1-8).

As the New Jerusalem City descends to earth, John puts in a climax, the final words or the sounds that come from the throne and from the One seated on the throne. These final sounds take much significance, for they are the words of the Covenant God speaking for his blessings and curses to the redeemed and the lost, respectively:

> "And I heard a loud voice from the throne saying, "Now the dwelling of God is with men, and he will dwell with

them. They will be his people, and God himself will be with them and be their God. He will wipe away every tear from their eyes. There will be no more death or mourning or crying or pain, for the old order of things has passed away." He who was seated on the throne said, "I am making all things new!" Then he said, "Write these words down, for these words are trustworthy and true." He said to me; "It is done. I am the Alpha and the Omega, the Beginning and the End. To him who is thirsty I will give to drink without cost from the spring of the water of life. He who overcomes will inherit all this, and I will be his God and he will be my son. But the cowardly, the unbelieving, the vile, the murderers, the sexually immoral, those who practice magic arts, the idolaters and all liars their place will be in the lake of burning sulfur. This is the second death" (Rev 21:3-8).

This review of the context of sounds surrounding Revelation 8:1 leads to the conclusion that heaven is a place of sounds and action. A note of importance for a world in which dissonant sounds and noises have become popular is the fact that the sounds of heaven are not meaningless sounds. In the first place they are the divine voice in words that proclaim the divine will. They are also words that proclaim the divine judgment - - words of vindication and retribution. In heaven one finds the seat of divine judgment. In the powerful vision of Daniel chapter 7, which describes the judgment against the beastly powers and the traitorous little horn, words are spoken to describe the divine seat of judgment, and these are later reflected in Revelation. Daniel says:

> "As I looked, thrones were set in place, and the Ancient of Days took his seat. His clothing was as white as snow; the hair of his head was like wool. His throne was flaming with fire, and its wheels were all ablaze. A river of fire was flowing, coming out from before him. Thousands attended

> him; ten thousand stood before him. The court was seated, and the books were opened" (Dan 7:9,10).
>
> "But the court will sit, and his [the little horn] power will be taken away and completely destroyed forever. Then the sovereignty, power and greatness of the kingdoms under the whole heaven will be handed over to the saints, the people of the Most High. His kingdom will be an everlasting kingdom, and all rulers will worship and obey him" (Dan 7:26, 27).

God speaks from heaven. Heaven is the seat of His rule and direction (Dan 2:18, 19, 44; Ezra 1:2; 5:11; Jn 1:9). Heaven is His throne and earth is His footstool (Isa 66:1; Rev 4:2; 20:11; Matt 5:34; Acts 7; 49). He is king over all the earth (Psa 42:2; Zech 14:9).

A fact that follows the conclusion is that the heavenly sounds are worship and praise sounds. The creatures in heaven are in a continuous act of worship to the divine. Johnson Oatman Jr. (1894) puts it beautifully:

> There is singing up in heaven such as we have never known,
> Where the angels sing the praises of the Lamb upon the throne;
> Their sweet harps are ever tuneful and their voices always clear,
> That we might be more like them while we serve our master here!
> Holy, holy, is what the angels sing,
> And I expect to help them make the courts of heaven ring;
> But when I sing redemption's story, they will fold their wings,
> For angels never felt the joys that our salvation brings.

In their worship sounds the heavenly creatures praise God for His works of creation. They sing of the sovereign (and providential) power of God. They sing of the Lamb that was slain from the foundation of the world. The life and death of Christ stands as a subject for constant praise. Their spontaneous sounds tell of the divine goodness. There is no time or theme in which they do not seek to glorify the Creator rather than the creature. Their sounds range from a moderate amen to a grand hallelujah. Their sounds seem to be more harmonious than dissonant. Since the field of sounds has been pursued in the long history of religion, and since there has never been a culture as conscious as we are with our electronic distortion of amplification, frequency and duration, a point that must be made is that the heavenly sounds of worship are not merely noises, of senseless emotions and attention to performance of stentorian musical styles, as we have in today's outrage. No, it is not the inelegant, mutinous, obtrusive, jabbing, autonomous, sounds of lawless lives. They are not part of the culture of melodrama that is intoned in the secularized earth where humanity is worshipped. The heavenly sounds are different. They are the sounds in which God is worshipped.

A third point to recognize is that the heavenly sounds are sounds of prayerful conversations. The voices of the "saints under the altar" can be heard in holy dialogue and reverberation. In the midst of their suffering (persecution) and their death, they ask, "How long, O lord, the Holy and true One, do you not judge and avenge our blood on those who live on the earth" (Rev 6:9-11). No word is immediately said, and so one might suspect that God is not about to respond, but as one follows the narrative one sees the actions of God in Christ as He brings the work of salvation to completion through Christ's return to earth the second time (Rev 6:17-19) to gather His saints unto Himself (Rev 20:4-6). Preceding the coming, the angels from heaven will hold the winds of strife in order that the servants of God might be sealed in their foreheads (Rev 7:1-3). In effect, when the saints pray, "How long, Sovereign Lord, holy and true, until you judge the inhabitants of the earth and avenge our blood," and the sweet incense ascends to God, God answers. He does not only answer by telling the saints to wait until their fellows should suffer like persecutions, but also by calling all of the heavenly host into action against the forces of iniquity. In this understanding God might resolve not to speak (Heb. *hasa*) or to speak quietly (Heb. *duma*). He might dispose to keep something secret (Gk. *sige*) as well as to make it manifest (Gk. *apocalypsis*). When God is silent, such silence is often followed by a great manifestation of power, such as happened in the creation when He spoke a great word, or in His acts of judgment when He pronounces a verdict.[48] We can conclude that God's silence or the heavenly silence is powerful. Through its manifestation "the mystery of God" is to be accomplished (Rev 10:7). But in His silence God is still in charge of the history of the world.

The further point might be made, then, that heaven is a place of constant activity. Such activity produces constant sounds--thunderous sounds and other sounds. From heaven angels are sent on continuous missions to earth. One Scripture says that the angels are ministering spirits sent forth to minister on the behalf of those who love God (Heb 1:13, 14). In the words of one songwriter, "The angels in heaven they have no time to spare."

The reality of heaven as a place of sounds is very assuring. Western humanity *dreads* silence. When God speaks, in creative, in commanding words and in words of judgment, they sense hope. When there is no voice, there is confusion. When the prayers of the saints are answered, there is joy. When there are no answers, there is dread of night and pain. When evil seems to be triumphing, there are feelings of despair, and questions are raised concerning the divine existence. This has been the theodicical challenge. But some persons have gone as far as to develop theologies of the "Death of God," arguing that God has left the world. With the latter rationalization they make their idols and parodize them, for

---

[48] Cf. The Analytical Greek Lexicon (1967), (Grand Rapids, MI: Zondervan).

they want to have a god who speaks to them. Only they find that the word they receive is their own word and not a word from heaven.

The solemn silence

The study of the heavenly sounds as they are reflected in Revelation is great, but there is a truth about God and heaven that we said causes the religious concern and the secular human being much fear: namely, that there is silence in heaven. Great attention is drawn to the reality of the silence, but few wish to even halt to observe it, and fewer still to interpret it. Therefore, there remains much to be said about the lack of appreciation for this silence. Although we argued that there were liturgical pauses and pace for change of action in the sounds of Revelation, we have not been able to find another explicit statement on silence. Revelation 8:1 is therefore quite significant. Building on some observations from a previous discussion, I note what Jon Paulien says:

The opening of the seventh seal results in only a simple statement to the effect that a brief silence occurs in heaven. The silence functions like a storm after a calm after the storm of destruction occasioned by Christ's Second Coming. A number of explanations have been offered to explain the meaning of this silence, but none has proved decisive. One possibility is that the silence is an announcement that the justice of God has been fully executed. This is based on textual statements that in the face of injustice God refuses to keep silent until justice have been served (Psa 50:3-6; Isa 65:6-7) . . . . Other possibilities for interpreting the silence of the seal include the end-time counterpart to the silence at the beginning (Gen 1:2; cf. Ezra 7:26-31); the silence of the universe as it watches the destruction of evil (in stark contrast to the celebration of Revelation 5); and the silence of the courtroom when the book is finally opened.[49]

Paulien's point does not note the meaning of the silence so much as it observes that silence actually appears in the midst of the heavenly sounds. Out of the solo voice of the divine, and the vocal, orchestral, choral and thunderous sounds of the heavenly beings come the "sound of silence." In the heavenly liturgical order there is praise, adoration, proclamation, and, in between, silence. As we have already noted, in Christian worship it is the Quakers, more than anyone else, who understand the ontological order of silence. They utilize it more than human words. In their liturgical order they speak of "silent worship." They demand that persons sit together for the silent reading of Scripture or other sacred literature, and only when the Spirit gives enlightenment can one comment upon or exegete the text being contemplated. Their understanding is that it is in silence that one can meet the reality of the divine most profoundly. God, they observe, is submerged in silence. Thus one who cannot listen to silence cannot hear God. The point for them is that to encounter God and heaven is to encounter silence. Their understanding might serve to indict the rest of the Christian community and much that is being done in contemporary praise worship with more sounds than silence. I shall leave this observation for another time, but here the point to be made clear is that even where there might not be the explicit note of silence in the liturgical order of Revelation, there is time and place for silence. Revelation 8:1 is distinct because it stands as the intermezzo in an orchestral recital before the grand finale. One might note again that it is followed by the blowing of trumpets (Rev 8:6ff), the sounds that in the time of Scriptural history called the Israelites to solemn days of worship, judgment and war (Lev 25:9), other days of judgment (Isa 18:3; Neh 4:20), and times of war (Jer 4:19; 51:27; Zeph 9:44). In Revelation trumpets (Rev 8:2,

---

[49] Jon. Paulien (1992), "The Seven Seals," in Symposium on Revelation, Book I, edited by Frank Holbrook (Silver Spring, MD: Biblical Research Institute), 237-238.

6-8, 10, 12; 9:1, 13; 11:15) introduce seven visions, and the heavenly voices heard by John often sound like trumpets (cf. 1:10; 4:1). The point here is that the silence stands in contrast to the blasting sounds. It is acute, incisive, overpowering, deadening, and unnatural. Although it may be a part of the even flow of things, yet, it seems disruptive, an aberrant.

The half-an-hour of silence

And not only is the time of silence palpable because of its unnaturalness and intensity, but its duration makes it challenging. Leon Morris states that, "Clearly it was a solemn and impressive moment." He does not spend time to focus on the meaning of the half an hour, but goes on to offer the fascinating explanation that the silence might be connected with the offering of the prayers of the saints (8:3-4) during which certain plagues are held back. Great cataclysms are held back while the saints pray. The praises of angels turn to silence so that the prayers of the saints may be heard. He also suggests that the judgments of God are about to begin, and there is solemn awe and silence at the power of God.[50]

But the half-an-hour is a challenge to any anxious heart. Time, as we know it, is mysterious and relative. Although it is a part of everyday life when we try to explain it, it baffles us. Thus when we face a car accident a half an hour is a long time. In the case of a plane crash, five minutes might be like a day. In the case of a computer crash a nano second is like eternity. Thus while five, ten, fifteen, thirty minutes might not seem like short time in abstract terms, when such is penetrated by silence it can be awesome, if not awful. Whatever is meant, one will never know if cultural explanations can resolve the problem of the half-an-hour of heavenly time. Some commentators try to resolve the problem by suggesting that the "half an hour" of silence is literal time.

---

[50] Leon Morris, (1987) Revelation: Tyndale New Testament Commentaries, (Grand Rapids, MI: Wm. B. Eerdmans), 116-117

Other commentators contend that it must be placed in the context of prophetic history. In the latter sense a time formula of a day for a literal year is used to calculate the time. "Half an hour" would mean a literal week. But some persons do not find warrant for the latter view.[51] My own view is that one might never know whether it is literal or prophetic time. One only has to follow through on the context of Revelation as a document of prophetic and apocalyptic history and say it is "heavenly" time. Heaven transforms time (*chronos*) into eternity (*kairos*). The half an hour of silence gives us an orientation to the relationship between the temporal (*chronos*) life and eternity (kairos). With God a thousand years are like a day that has just passed, or like a watch in the night (Psa 90:4 cf. 2 Pet 3:8). Thus for me silence speaks profoundly of a new direction of time. As C. Norman Kraus says:

> The movement toward the consummation of history comes through kairotic [instead of chronotic] events which occur in God's timing and by God's power. . . The eschatological consummation is a kairotic event, which ends history, as we know it, perhaps as the bursting of the cocoon ends the life of the larvae. The biblical apocalyptic writers visualized the end as a catastrophic climax of both social events (wars and social chaos) and natural events earthquakes, drought and disturbances in the sky). They picture it as a destruction of the old and a recreation of the new (2 Pet 3:8ff). In more recent times some have associated it with atomic disaster. But these events in themselves occurring as they do in temporal sequence do not describe the character and meaning of the kairotic reality.[52]

---

[51] F. D. Nichol, ed. (1980), Seventh-day Adventist Bible Commentary, (Hagerstown, MD: Review and Herald), 787.

[52] C. Norman Krauss (1991), God Our Savior: Theology in a Christological Mode (Scotsdale, Penn.: Herald Press), 204.

We shall say much more of the time of silence and the divine sovereignty in the discussion that follows. Here we note that this silence emphasizes that what has gone before in history carries urgency for the ominous event that is to come. In effect, this silent time is "lead time," which gives us a special orientation to our future. The time of silence chains the events of time and eternity together.[52] In the figure that follows, I shall try to illustrate what I understand of the dynamics of that which precedes and that which follows this time of silence, for the silence is not an empty moment, but a moment that leads to a new reality.

[52] I am indebted to Edward T. Hall in his published work of 1973, The Silent Language, for the above insights on time and silence.

The moment of silence

At the completion of creation, God declared that the creation was very good; thereupon, all entered into a moment of silence (Gen 2:1-3). It was the institution of the great Sabbath rest, on which occasion the morning stars sang together for joy (Job 38:7). The silence was followed by a magnificent worship service. Something awesome had occurred.

Soon afterward sin, with all its mystery, entered the universe. One hardly needs to guess. The music stopped. "There was war in heaven. Michael and His angels fought against the dragon, and the dragon and his angels fought back. But he was not strong enough, and they lost their place in heaven. The dragon was hurled down - - that ancient serpent called the devil, or Satan who leads the whole world astray. He was hurled to the earth, and his angels with him" (Rev 12:7-9). John, who gives us this description of the drama, does not tell us what happened between the casting of Satan out of heaven into the earth and the loud voice heard in heaven for the victory of Michael over Satan (Rev 12:10-12). Something so awful had taken place, and there is little detail of it. When something so awful has taken place there is a usual silence (cf. Gen 3:8).

At the death of respectable friends and public servants there are moments of silence, because something *mysterious* and supposedly *stupid* has happened. Mysterious and stupid because in our human frame we cannot interpret death, though we want to interpret it. The best interpretation of death is to stand before it in silence. We stop the music as the heavenly creatures did at the fall. And although we sing dirges, our songs are mixed with silent groans. In effect, we are just trying to make sense of a senseless thing. Christian hope rests on the fact that it knows that only God really has the answer for death and can speak as He does to John in Revelation. "Write," he says, "Blessed are the dead who die in the Lord from now on. Yes . . . they will rest from their labor, for their deeds follow them" (Rev 14:13-14). He will descend from heaven with a shout, with the voice of the Archangel and with the trumpet of God (1 Thess 4:16). He will ask death, "Where, O death, is your victory? Where, O death, is your sting?" (1 Cor 15:55).

After the silent pause at the entrance of sin, the plan of salvation was revealed to the heavenly inhabitants. Again one can imagine that there was silence. Christ the Lamb was to leave heaven and come to live and die for us humans on earth (Gen 3:15; Phil 2:5-11). This was an awesome and an awful time. The coming of the Son of God to live in our world and die for us was not something that would happen later and then pass away and disappear. The coming of the Son of God to earth would make Him the Son of Man.[54] That was something no angel could understand. I have imagined that for a moment they must have been silent.

When Christ prayed in the Garden of Gethsemane there was a moment of silence. He prayed, but, for a moment, heaven seemed cut off from Him. God did not answer. Christ felt God had abandoned Him. Darkness encircled Him when He cried, "My Father, if it is possible, let this cup pass from me; yet not what I want, but what you want"(Matt 26:39). Then an angel came and strengthened Him (Lk 22:42, 43). The same drama happened while He was on the cross. In Matthew's version, in the darkness He cried, "My God, My God, Why have you forsaken me" (Matt 27:46). According to Luke, "It was about the sixth hour, darkness came over the whole land until the ninth hour, for the sun stopped shining, and the curtain of the temple was torn in two. Jesus called out in a loud voice, 'Father into your hand I commit my spirit.' When He had said this He breathed His last" (Lk 23:44-46). Whether the heavenly silence continued for three hours or for brief moments within the three hours, one cannot say. What is certain is that there was an inexplicable silence. Something awesome and

---

[54] Karl Barth (Latest impression 1989), Church Dogmatics: V:2: The Doctrine of Reconciliation (Edinburgh: T&T Clark), 35.

awful had taken place. From the cross Christ cries to His Father. Thielike says, "He grasps at the One who seemed to have forsaken Him. He speaks to the One who apparently does not hear. He counts on the One who seems not to exist."[55] And such a One hears Him and answers through the resurrection on Sunday morning with a violent earthquake and an angel who rolls away the stone (Matt 28:2). Having passed through the grave, Christ ascends to the right hand of God where He becomes The Great Intercessor for us. This, we said, is the great subject of the worship in the heavenly sanctuary, which is clearly stated in Revelation 4, 5.

When the intercessory activity of Christ is ended, He will leave the sanctuary in heaven to return to the earth once again, and there will be "silence for the space of half an hour." Again something *awful* and *awesome* is about to take place. The trumpet will then sound out the Second Coming (1Thess 4:16), and the eschatological judgment will be consummated (Rev 8:6ff). The half an hour of silence takes us from the Second Coming to the final consummation.

The point being made that will be expanded in the next aspect of our discussion is that God has the last word. Within His silence there is a powerful subject matter. Whether it is considered a mystery or a secret, God has a word, and that word must come from silence.

---

[55] Helmut Thielike (1962), The Silence of God (Grand Rapids, MI.: Wm. B. Eerdmans), 75.

God has the last word.
He has spoken through His Word.
What He has promised, He will perform.
He has said, He will judge the world in righteousness,
and He will perform it.

III

WHAT HAPPENS WHEN GOD IS SILENT

God speaks from heaven

God speaks (Rev 1:1,2). "God speaks in one way and in two though people do not perceive it" (Job 33:14). "God the Lord speaks and summons the earth from the rising of the sun to the setting" (Psa 30:1). God speaks from heaven (Dan 4:31). He communicates with us mortals in words of approval and rebuke (Heb 11:4). He speaks a first and a last word (Rev 1:8 cf. Heb 1:1). But God does not always speak in words (Rev 1:2); sometimes He speaks through acts (Deut 3:24), in omens, in figures and in the silent motions of nature.[56] There is no speech, there are no words, the voice is not heard (Psa 19:3). Since "action speaks louder than words," God manifests Himself in ordinary things of life, in epiphanic and theophanic appearances (in the things of nature), through the words of Scripture, and through His Son Jesus Christ (Heb 1:1-3). This is the most authentic understanding we have of God in the book of Revelation (cf. Rev 1:1,2; 10:20) and in all of Scripture. In the title of the book of Revelation we are introduced to the double understanding that God manifests Himself (speaks about Himself) and also hides (sometimes He refuses to speak about) Himself in mystery. As Abraham Heschel says, "The mystery of meaning is silent."[57] The Greek name for *Revelation*, *Apocalypse*, means, "*to uncover* that

---

[56] Max Picard (1952), The World of Silence (Chicago: H. Regency), 76.
[57] Abraham J. Heschel (1955), God in Search of Man: A Philosophy of Judaism (New York: Farrar, Straus and Giroux), 108.

which *has been covered,*" and it also means "*to disclose*" and "*to hide"* at the same time.

Fig 3:1

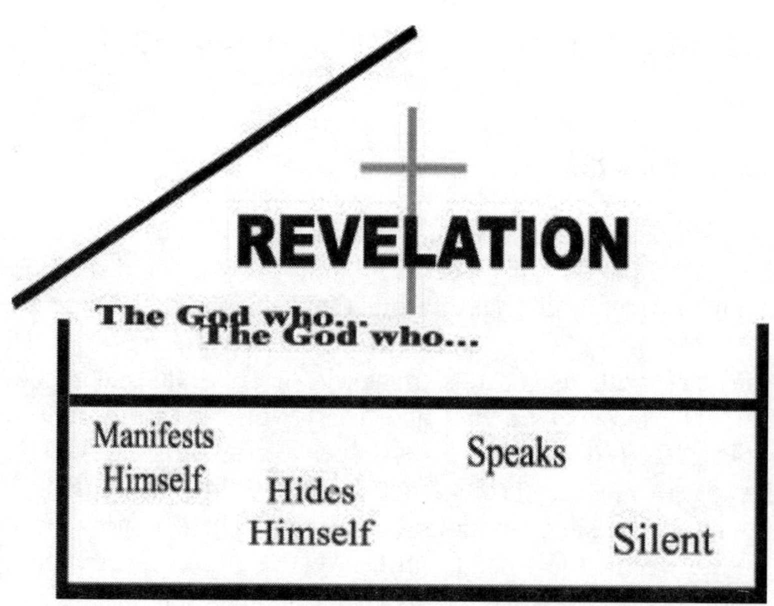

Revelation provides understanding for those who are willing to see and hear, while it remains covered for those who are unwilling to hear. The words of Jesus recorded in the Gospels of Mark and Matthew note that to the children of God has been given the privilege of knowing the mysteries of the kingdom of God, while to others it has not been given so that seeing they may not see and hearing they may not hear and that they may not understand and be saved (Mk 4:11,12; Matt 13: 11-13).

From the testimony that John is given to bear of what he has "heard" and "seen" and "touched" of God's Word (1 Jn 1:1), John says, blessed is the one who reads aloud the words of the prophecy, and blessed are those who hear and keep what is written in it (Rev 1:3). "Let everyone who has ears to hear, listen to what the Spirit is saying to the churches" Rev 2:7, 17, 29; 3:6, 13, 22). He speaks about the loud voice that he heard like a trumpet blast behind him (Rev 1:10). And he speaks of "the words of the one who holds the seven stars in his right hand, who walks among the seven golden lampstands" (Rev 2:1), "the words of the first and the last, who was dead and came to life" (Rev 2:8), "the words of him who has the sharp two-edged sword (Rev 2:12), "the words of the Son of God, who has eyes like a flame of fire, and whose feet are like burnished bronze" (Rev 2:18), "the words of him who has the seven spirits of God and the seven stars" (Rev 3:1), "the words of the holy One, who has the keys of David, who opens and no one will shut, who shuts and no one opens" (Rev 3:7), and "the words of the Amen, the faithful and true witness, the origin of God's creation" (Rev 3:14). After making his observations about the resonant sounds, John then makes his contrasting observation that the one who has spoken is reduced to silence (Rev 8:1).[58]

Before speaking again of the puzzle of the above silence, let us take up some traditional theological observations, namely that the eternal God is the God who speaks and acts for Himself. This is how God is known. From the perspective of a systematic theology, He speaks through the Bible, He speaks through nature and history, He speaks through human experience, and He speaks through His Son, Jesus Christ as the Living Word.

The Bible as the word of God

One of the assertions of theology is that the Bible is the word of God. The understanding is that what is written in the Bible is what God says. Prophets, sages and apostles who wrote in

---

[58] Cf. Samuel Terrien (1978), The Elusive Presence (New York: Harper and Row). Terrien discusses in an effective manner how in theophanic appearances of the divine the cosmic noise is followed by the presence. The presence happens in the quiet such as in the case of Elijah on Mount Horeb. In effect, there is a rhythm between speech and silence.

the Bible prefaced their words with phrases like "God said," "God spoke," and "the word of the Lord came to me saying." It was their conviction that their word was the divine message. The New Testament writers spoke of the Old Testament as the word of Scripture, meaning that it was the word of the Lord (cf. 1 Cor 10:10; Rom 3:2; 9:17; 15:4; Acts 7:38). The New Testament understanding that God had been speaking through the authors of Scripture is stated clearly:

> All Scripture is inspired by God and is useful for teaching, for reproof, for correction, and for training in righteousness, so that everyone who belongs to God may be proficiently equipped for every good work. (11 Tim 3:16, 17).

> Because no prophecy ever came by human will, but holy men moved by the Holy Spirit spoke from God. (2 Pet 1:21).

Bible interpreters have sought to comment upon the above words using various hermeneutical approaches. On the one extreme they have argued that the Bible is the very words of God unmixed with human words. This is what they mean when they say God verbally inspires the Bible.[59] At the other extreme there is the assumption that the Bible is a human word unaffected by any miraculous intervention of God. That means that it is naturalistic, evolutionary and totally controlled by the human historical process. The latter interpreters feel that they can tear back the

[59] There are Fundamentalists who argue that in approaching Scripture one can expect to find the literal words of God. In the English-speaking world there is even the conviction that the King James Version has fallen from heaven. To use any other version is to do violence to the divine. I question this approach.

mystery of the Bible and make available the word of God.[60] In contrast to both extremes are those who affirm Scripture as the usual normative medium through which one may hear God speaking. They do not dispose of critical interpretations, but feel that such interpretations can only be trusted as they work from the perspective of critical faith, instead of critical suspicion. In effect, they approach the Scripture with the spirit of submission and trust that it is the medium for bearing the mystery of the divine word. As Hans Urs Von Balthasar says, "The word of God is not an empty dictate to which man adds meaning and content." [61]

As Jesus became incarnate in humanity, so the Bible incarnates God's words. For while the inspired human speaks, the Divine is speaking at the same time. This means that what is written is both divine and human. In the latter sense the grammatical and historical construction has to be reckoned with, yet the reality of the Transcendent Spirit that brought or brings relevance to the words must not be overlooked. The latter view, to which I am sympathetic, is the view held by many of the best

---

[60] For nearly two centuries now science and critical reason have dominated the field of research. The methods used in these fields came to dominate everything, not least the study of Scripture. Many hours are spent poring over the source and tradition of the Scripture and very little on the message. In the most extreme form of this method, God has nothing to say, for human beings have the last word. The end of this method has been approaching all of Scripture with a "hermeneutic of suspicion." My own conviction is that a historico-critical method can be helpful to identify the sources, forms, and context of Scripture, but that such a method has the fundamental flaw of not trusting the Spirit of God who inspired the thoughts of the scriptural authors and instructed them to write down the message.

[61] Hans Urs Von Balthasar, Translated by John Dury, (1971), The Theology of Karl Barth (New York: Holt, Rinehart & Winston), 87, 88.

scholars within the biblical tradition.[62] Martin Luther, for example, who saw the Scripture as central to his thinking, and who never speculated whether the Scripture contained the word of God, worked hard to rescue the Church from scholastic tradition. Of him, Jaroslav Pelikan, one of the best contemporary analysts of Luther, says that Luther spoke of "the Word of God" as "the speech of God" or "the God who speaks." For Pelikan, Luther characterized the God of the Bible not only as "one who created by his power" and "redeemed by His love, but He did what He did through His speech." Pelikan also argues that Luther frequently warned against any picture of God that would paint Him in remote and self-contained isolation. Luther's view is that it is in the very nature of God to speak: thus God is never speech-less. The point is that "The speech of God was as eternal as God Himself, and was God Himself" (cf. Jn 1:1). The God of Christian faith was one who had a voice, an eternal Speech. This voice and eternal Speech of God was the cosmic sense of the term "'Word of God.'"[63]

For John Calvin there was a profound conviction that the Bible is "the Word of God." Calvin often insisted that the two great sources by which God speaks are the outward universe and the Scripture, but he gave priority to the voice of God in Scripture; for, he argued, only through Scripture can we know God as the

[62] In this third view the idea is that the thoughts of every biblical author were inspired. With such inspiration they were able to speak the divine wisdom, love, truth, commandments, gospel, give the rebuke and say all the things on which we build doctrine. To hear God speak through this inspired word demands the listening ear and the humble heart. In a word, only the person of faith and prayer can hear God speak through the biblical word. This view does not argue for verbal inspiration; it argues for personal inspiration, but it does not say like Emil Brunner and his heirs that the personal inspiration is only a relational event or an encounter experience. Cf. Emil Brunner (1943), The Divine-Human Encounter (Philadelphia: Westminster Press). The word of inspiration is propositional truth and the relational experience. As I understand Paul in Romans 15:4, the Scripture was written to teach and to bring encouragement, so that the believer can bring the witness of grace.

[63] Jaroslav Pelikan (1959), Luther the Expositor: Introduction to the Reformers Exegetical Writings (Saint Louis, MO: Concordia Publishing House), 48-68.

Redeemer. In contradiction to the views of his time, Calvin also argued that an understanding about God does not come through the Church per se or through any discernible human qualities, but out of the reality of the word and the Spirit. The word and the Spirit work together to make clear the voice of God.[64]

For Zwingli, the Bible is the word of God because God has spoken through it. As God's word, it brings light where there is merely human light or the darkness of error. Because the Scripture comes from the Spirit, everything must yield to it. The doctrine of God is never formed more clearly than when it is declared by God himself and by God's word. The Scripture has its clarity because of God, who comes before the Scripture. In order to challenge the view that the words of the popes, the fathers and the doctors of the Roman Catholic Church were more legitimate than the word of God, Zwingli argued that the human word must yield to the word of God and not the word of God to the human word. He stated that he was not against the doctors of the Church as long as they conformed to the word of God.[65]

My point here is to assert that if Luther, Calvin or Zwingli were alive today they would be shocked to see how many of their followers have rationalized away the voice of God in Scripture. In many circles today the whole or part of Scripture is dispensable; its authority is challenged, and more credence is given to the word of humanity than the word of God in Scripture.

The creation as the transcendent speech of God

Even as God speaks in Scripture, so also God speaks to humanity through the creative works of nature. In the works of nature we not only find a word, but a speech act. The Hebrews understood this when they used *dabar* to speak of the divine act of

---

[64] Cf. John Calvin (1950 ed.), Institute of the Christian Religion Vol. 1, Edited by John McNeil (Philadelphia: The Westminster Press).

[65] See W. P. Stephens (1986), The Theology of Hulrych Zwingli (Oxford: The Clarendon Press).

creating. Jacques Ellul states that God's word is the equivalent of action it is power as it acts, and His word does not fail to have effect. In His word the Divine works par excellence as He did at creation.[66] One Psalmist says: "By the word of the Lord the heavens were made, and all their host by the breath of his mouth" (Psa 33:6). God creates through His word. There was no struggle for God to create. God spoke and things came to pass.[67] But it is of interest that the loudest word in nature comes to those who love God. They are given supernatural insight. The same things of nature conceal God from those who are blinded by the drunkenness of the world. Jacques Chevalier interprets Pascal to say that often enough those who look at nature fasten upon it and make it the final goal of their desires instead of seeing in it the symbol and signs which represent God.[68] God speaks in the order and harmony of nature and in its brokenness. Paul says it this way:

> For the wrath of God is revealed from heaven against all ungodliness and wickedness of those who by their wickedness suppress the truth. For what can be known about God is clear to them. Ever since the creation of the world his eternal power and divine nature, invisible though they are, have been understood and seen through the things he has made. So they are without excuse; for though they knew God they did not honor him as God or give thanks to him, but they became futile in their thinking, and their senseless minds were darkened. Claiming to be wise they became fools; and they exchanged the glory of the immortal God for images resembling a mortal human being or birds or four-footed animals or reptiles . . . . (Romans 1:18-22).

We can be thankful today that even though the arrogance of humanity has run roughshod against God and even though many in

---

[66] Jacques Ellul (1985), The Humiliation of the Word (Grand Rapids, MI: Wm. B. Eerdmans, Pub. Co.), 49.
[67] Ibid.
[68] Jacques Chevalier (1930), Pascal (New York: Longman's, Green & Co.), 76.

our scientific culture have stopped listening to God, there is evidence that there is a returning to the recognition of the divine voice in the things of nature. This is not pantheism (namely that God is in everything) or panentheism (that everything is God), nor process thinking (that God is part of life's processes). It is, rather, the recognition that all of life can be celebrated as the divine handiwork (Psa 19; 24; Rev 4; 11). A point of emphasis must be made here, that raised by Abraham Heschel, namely, that science cannot silence God, because scientific terms are meaningless to the spirit that raises the questions, meaningless to the concern for truth, greater than the world that science is engaged in exploring. God is not the only subject that is inaccessible to science; the issue of the origin of reality remains immune to it. There are aspects of the given reality that are congruous with the categories of scientific logic, while there are aspects of reality that are inaccessible to it. Even some aspects and concepts of our own thinking are impregnable to analysis.[69] So there needs not be any pretense that we can have control of all knowledge.

What has been said is not to suggest that science does not contribute to the voice of God but it is to make the point that the world remains an enigma to the minds that only work by speculation and scientific theoretization.[70] For only in faith might one enter into the mystery of God.

God speaks to us through human experience

Phyllis Hobe points to a significant source through which God speaks when she raises the question:

> Is it ever possible to hear God? I used to wonder about that. I know people who have heard God speak, but no two of them can agree on what they heard. Some said his voice was gentle as a breeze. Some shrank back from his

[69] Abraham J. Heschel (1955), God in Search of Man: A Philosophy of Judaism (New York: Farrar, Straus and Giroux), 108.
[70] Ibid., 111.

> thunderous tones. Some said that he did not speak in a voice at all but in a thought that entered unbidden into the mind. And some said that he spoke through an event – or through another person.[71]

Hobe is not being derisive; I believe she does agree that God speaks though Scripture, the Spirit of Prophecy, the voice of conscience, direct voice, the counsel of others who have expertise in an area of concern, and in prayer experiences. But she also knows that sometimes as humans we fail to hear the voice of God. Her point about deepening one's relationship with God in order to hear God is well taken, then. Many persons have reported that the speech and silence of God only becomes effective to them through personal relationships, through trials and tribulations, and through sickness and death. The witness of the Spirit of God in human life is therefore of special importance, and it can be heard by its bearers and seen by many observers. For example, the kings of ancient Babylon and Medo-Persia observed concerning Daniel that the spirit of the holy gods was in him, and no mystery was too difficult for him (cf. Dan 4:9; 5:11). They understood that it was the voice of God that spoke the wisdom that was evident in Daniel. This same Spirit continuously calls the world to the recognition of the divine will. Thus in Revelation we read, "The Spirit and the Bride say 'Come!' And let him who hears say 'Come!'" (Rev 22:17). And in Hebrews, "The Spirit says, 'Today if you will hear his voice, do not harden your heart'" (Heb 3:7). All of the scriptural authors have been insistent on the voice of the Spirit when they argue that the Spirit is available to be "poured out on all flesh" (Joel 2:28ff; Acts 2:16ff) and "into our hearts" (Gal 4:6). In this way the Spirit dwells in us who are the divine temples (1 Cor 6:19, 20) and speaks to us. There are those who make themselves deaf to the words that God has sent by his Spirit (Zech 7:12) and who in their rebellion have sinned against the Holy Spirit (cf. Matt 12:32; Lk 12:10). They have not listened to the Spirit

---

[71] Phyllis Hobe (1982, 1987), The Wonder of Prayer (Carmel, New York: Guidepost), 72.

who searches the things of God and who interprets for them the divine will, but have lived by their own wisdom and desires. This is why our world is filled with so many persons who are called unspiritual (*sarkikois*) beings (cf. 1 Cor 3:1). Abraham Heschel says correctly that it is the evil in human beings that silences the voice of God. The voice of the Lord cries in the wilderness (Isa 40:3) and in the cities of our land (Mic 6:9), but it is not heard.[72] Those who listen to God's voice are called spiritual beings (pneumatikois) (1 Cor 3:1ff). They acknowledge that there is transcendence. They know that there is the ineffable. They are therefore willing to let God speak and do some explaining, in which case they go to God and ask in faith, what do these things mean?

God speaks to us through world history

Not only is God's voice heard through human experience, but also his voice is heard through world history. Max Picard says that when humanity is no longer under the direction of the Word, history and events undertake to teach humanity truths that can no longer reach humanity by the word.[73] It is in this direction that we assert that the Divine speaks through the history of creation and through the history of salvation. He spoke in patriarchal history in the recital of the covenant promises, He spoke in the deliverance of Israel out of Egyptian slavery, He spoke in prophetic and apostolic history, He spoke in the rise and fall of empires, He speaks in contemporary history and will continue to speak about the things that will happen in the future, to the end of time (cf. Rev 1:19; 4:1). A point that can be made from the biblical historical view is that God is in control of history. God is the Lord of history.

---

[72] Abraham J. Heschel (1955), God in Search of Man: A Philosophy of Judaism (New York: Farrar, Straus and Giroux), 141.

[73] Max Picard (1952), The World of Silence (Chicago: H. Regency), 77.

The above point is made in all of Scripture, but I am fascinated by how it is treated in the books of Daniel and Revelation. Here I only make reference to Daniel because his is the first of the two great apocalyptic books in Scripture. In the first chapter of the book it is announced that the Lord lets Jehoiakim and the covenant people fall into the hands of Nebuchadnezzer and his army. But God allows the faithful to the covenant, namely Daniel and his companions, to find favor with the palace master and ultimately with the king. In the tests that Daniel and his companions face in the first and subsequent chapters, God manifests himself in ways that have the heathen king and his subjects testifying of the power of God. In the second chapter, God speaks of the future in prophetic history when He gives Nebuchadnezzer a dream that the king cannot remember. But in love and mercy God reveals the dream: in the midst of the succession of kingdoms, the God of heaven will set up a kingdom which will never be destroyed. In the third chapter Nebuchadnezzar defies God by setting up an image to proclaim his own eternity, and when he makes a blazing furnace to punish the Hebrew worthies who resisted his call to worship his image, Daniel's God walks in the midst of the fire to show Nebuchadnezzar that the determination of life in the present and the future is in the Divine hands. In the fourth chapter God continues to speak against the arrogance of King Nebuchadnezzar. When the king fails to listen to the Divine voice, God issues a decree, and the king becomes mentally ill. For seven years the king leaves his throne; then he humbles himself and worships the God of heaven. In the fifth chapter God pronounces judgment through the mysterious hand that writes the solemn words *Mene, Mene, Tekel, Peres* upon the wall. And in these words the fate of Babylon is settled. In the sixth chapter Daniel shows how Darius comes to learn of the divine power in guiding the history of nations and in personally intervening in human lives. Here God preserves Daniel by sealing the lions' mouths. The jealous deception of those who sought to destroy Daniel is made evident. In the end Darius praises the God of heaven who endures forever. From the seventh chapter through the eleventh chapter the succession of kingdoms is restated in a number of dreams and visions. The point that is made in every dream and vision is that the divine rules. Against the little horn, which uses arrogant words against the God of heaven, God sits in judgment and proclaims His authority. When the horn seeks to destroy "the Beautiful land" and desecrate the temple, its times are limited (Daniel 8:14). At the end of the historical stage the divine speaks words of judgment against the little horn, the arrogant kings, and all the forces of opposition who speak against God (cf. Dan 11:45).

Throughout the whole book Daniel receives many messages of reassurance that the God of heaven will enter into the history of the world. There are some aspects of the future history that were not made known to Daniel: he therefore asks God for explanations. But God tells him, "Go your way, Daniel, because the words are closed up and sealed until the time of the end" (Daniel 12:9). The point is emphasized, as in all of Scripture, that God is in charge of history and speaks a prophetic word to reassure his people that the future belongs to him.

Old Testament scholar G. Ernest Wright correctly argues that biblical theology is the confessional recital of the redemptive acts of God in a particular history, because His history is the chief medium of revelation, and that God acted and also spoke in numerous ways, especially by certain interpreters.[74] Using this lead, Oscar Cullmann and many other scholars of his time spoke of this historical revelation as "salvation history" (German, *Heilesgeschite*). From their assertions an extensive debate ensued between theologians as to whether there were two histories in the world or whether there was one history. And, in response, theologians like Wolfhart Pannenberg sought to resolve the debate by arguing that history is not two but one - - that the divine revelation takes place in the "totality" of history. Pannenberg sees

[74] G. Ernest Wright (1952), God Who Acts: Biblical Theology as Recital: Studies in Biblical Theology 8 (Chicago: Henry Regnery).

history as "God's master act." He says that no one act of history reveals (or speaks for) God, but that all of history does.[75]

While Pannenberg makes a masterful observation, he dismisses the profound moments of the divine manifestations in which persons encounter the divine and are transformed. He also misses the point that some moments of history are demonized. History, in the sense that it is understood in the Scripture, is cosmic and local, communal and individual, global and regional. This means that there will be moments in history in which it will be easy to hear the voice of God and there are moments when it might be difficult to hear the voice of God.[76] I shall return to expand on this idea when I speak of why God is sometimes silent, but here I simply note that the joy of life will come to the believer who recognizes "that God is the One who ultimately sets the boundaries in which we live and move and have our being."[77] The point is this: we must not go through life thinking that we are just part of a great scheme of things, but we must recognize that in a real and personal sense God encounters us with a personal word in history. God is Lord of history and is also involved in the circumstances of our personal lives through which we witness to His word.

God speaks to us through the Spirit of Prophecy

Most of what we have mentioned in the above leads us to consider the Spirit of Prophecy, for the prophetic Spirit bears testimony to the Word of God (Rev 19:10). The Biblical understanding is that the prophets saw themselves as "God's mouthpiece." The Hebrew word for prophet is *nabi* and means "spokesperson." The prophets became the mouthpiece of God. From their participation in the council of God they were able to

---

[75] Wolfhart Pannenberg, ed. (1968), Revelation as History (New York: Macmillan).

[76] Jeffery Hopper (1987), Understanding II: Reinterpreting Christian Faith for Changing Worlds (Philadelphia: Fortress Press), 49-67.

[77] John K. Roth, "The Silence of God" Faith and Philosophy 1:4 (October 1984): 407-418.

come forth with God's messages of warning, rebuke, encouragement and comfort for God's people. Old Testament prophets like Jeremiah, Isaiah and Ezekiel made the point that God has put His words into the prophets' mouths (Jerm 1:5-9; Isa 6:8ff; Ezek. 2). For Amos, "the Lord will not do anything, except He reveals His secrets to His servants the prophets" (Amos 3:7). In the New Testament we are told that in ancient times, God spoke unto the fathers through the prophets (Heb 1:1), and that no prophecy of Scripture is of one's own private interpretation but that men and women who spoke for God were moved by the Holy Spirit (2 Pet 1:21). Of interest is the fact that the Scripture indicts those prophets who prophesied "lying dreams" and saw false visions (cf. Jer 23:32). Without hearing a word from God they multiplied words, offered their ideas and opinions and beguiled their hearers in the ways of destruction (cf. Ez 13:9; 22:28).[78] The New Testament tells us that as the last days press upon us the number of false messiahs and false prophets will multiply (cf. Matt 24:11; 2 Pet 2:1; 1 Jn 4:1). They will produce 'signs" and "wonders" and use them to deceive the elect, if such were possible (Matt 24:24; Mk 13:22; Rev 16:14). Their greatest activity of deception will be carried out among the rulers of the earth who are to be gathered together for the great war of the day of God (Rev 16: 14). In contrasting the true prophets with the false, C. Norman Kraus states that, as spokespersons for God, the prophets were provided the ground and courage to challenge the king, the corporate head of the nation. Such God-awareness marked the authentic prophets. By contrast the self-identity of the court prophets merged with that of the nation. They identified God's voice with that of their national leaders and spoke what the kings wanted to hear. The prophets of the Lord, on the other hand,

---

[78] Jacques Ellul (1985), The Humiliation of the Word (Grand Rapids, MI: Wm. B. Eerdmans), 109.

distinguished between the voice of God and the national ego, and they spoke as individual representatives of God to the nation.[79]

A passing comment about many who are being called prophets today might be worthwhile when one notices that their sources do not match up to the word of God in Scripture. They might be using every phenomenon in nature to speak and predict a prophetic word, but when judged in the light of Scripture it is clear that "there seems to be no light in them." Heretical theologies are the natural result of the cultural prophetic phenomenon. One must therefore be reminded of the constant instruction of Jesus to his disciples to be "beware" of false prophets (Matt 7:15).

God speaks to us though Jesus Christ – the Living Word

To name the ultimate way that God speaks, we quote the full text of Hebrews 1:1,2:

> In the past God spoke to our fore-fathers through the prophets at many times and in various ways, but in these last days he has spoken to us by His Son whom he has appointed heir of all things, and through whom He made the universe. The Son is the radiance of God's glory and the exact representation of His being, sustaining all things by His powerful word.

Many translators tell us that the phrase "in various ways" should read that God has spoken "in a fragmentary way," but that in these last days God has spoken to us in a clear way, His One (Unique) Son. In this vein, William Barclay says that the prophets were the friends of God, while Jesus was the Son of God. Also meaning that if one wants to hear the most distinguishable word of God one must listen to Jesus Christ.[80] For Max Picard, Christ came directly from silence into the world. Before, the whole world was between silence and language – but with his coming the world

---

[79] C. Norman Kraus (1993), The Community of the Spirit (Waterloo, Ontario: Herald Press), 45.

[80] William Barclay (1976), The Letter to the Hebrews: The Daily Study Bible (Philadelphia: Westminster Press), 14.

of mythology was exploded and deprived of its significance and value.[81]

John's testimony in Revelation is that any ultimate revelation must come from Jesus Christ who is the Word of God, the Faithful and True Witness, who carries the two-edged sword in his mouth (Rev 2:13). Jesus Christ only speaks that which God gives to him to show to his servants what must take place. John says, Jesus made things known to him by sending his angel so that servant John, who with the seven churches (cf. Rev 1:1,2).

The fact here is that we have come full circle back to our opening statement, namely that God speaks, and ultimately so, in Jesus Christ. He speaks a creative word, a providential word, and now we can say he speaks a *salvific* word. I review a few thoughts of Jacques Ellul, whom I have quoted often, in regard to the word. Ellul says that the God who speaks to humanity is "God with humanity." To say that the Word was made incarnate means that God manifested himself, and that a proclamation has been given in Jesus Christ. "The invisible God came as a *word*." Ellul is emphatic about the fact that during his earthly ministry Jesus only spoke; He did not do things. Ellul explains his point by stating that Jesus did miracles, but these were only signs of the Word. The miracles were much less than the Word. He also says, "Jesus only spoke, he wrote nothing." He wrote only once on the ground and the words were soon erased, but when He told the woman taken in adultery, "Your sins are forgiven," the woman was liberated by the word. Since Jesus bears in Himself the Word of God, He can say, "I am the truth," "I am the life," "I am the way" (Jn 14:6). Jesus is the truth. He raises the question of truth about God and settles it in what He says.[82] Though I find Ellul's thesis to be fascinating, I do not seek to defend or deny it, except to say that in Jesus God has spoken and has done so explicitly. The most important point to be

---

[81] Max Picard (1952), The World of Silence (Chicago: H. Regency), 77.
[82] Jacques Ellul (1985), The Humiliation of the Word (Grand Rapids, MI: Wm. B. Eerdmans), 55, 56.

recited, from a Christian perspective, is that Jesus is God's last word to the world. Thus to "listen" to him and "act" on his word is to receive salvation.

God speaks and may choose not to speak, but idols are dumb

Whether God speaks through the Bible, creation, human experience, world history, the Spirit of Prophecy, through Jesus Christ or any other medium, what is clear is that God speaks. God can speak for Himself and has spoken for Himself. To say God speaks is not to make an anthropomorphic statement about God. Jacques Ellul notes the fact that if the phrase "God speaks" were just an expression, it would not be constant throughout all nine or ten centuries. He is focusing, of course, on the reality that God speaks in Jesus Christ as He speaks through the Holy Spirit. For he notes that the language God speaks is not just ordinary speech, but it is the spiritual language of life with a person. The view here is that when we hear God's word in Christ we are face to face with God and are therefore in contact with the First Word and the Last Word (Jn 1).[83] The speaking God is different from any dumb idol. Edward F. Markquart argues that the very word *idol* connotes deafness, dumbness, silence, and inability to speak, whereas the very nature of God is that He has a voice.[84] God hears, God sees, God speaks and He expects His people to listen and respond to Him. In both Bible Testaments the people of God who apostatized are derided for their deafness; they have turned aside from God to worship "dumb" idols and have thus committed themselves to all kinds of falsehoods (cf. Jer 10:5; 1 Cor 12:2).

One of the classic stories of the Bible that mocks those who listen to falsehood is that of Elijah on Mount Carmel confronting the prophets of Baal. The story picks up when Elijah is instructed by God to present himself to Ahab and advise him that

[83] Ibid.

[84] Edward Markquart (1985), Quest For Better Preaching: Resources for Renewal in the Pulpit (MN: Augsburg), 76.

the three and one half year drought on the land will be abated. On the way to present himself to Ahab, Elijah meets Obadiah, the servant of Ahab whom Elijah sends to tell Ahab that he, Elijah, is present. Obadiah is fearful for his life because he has acted as a true servant of God by resisting Ahab's order to kill all of the prophets of God. He is fearful to follow Elijah's order because he thinks that by the time he reaches the king Elijah will be spirited away. But with assurance from Elijah, Obadiah goes to tell Ahab and Ahab goes out to meet Elijah. Ahab's immediate question is, "Are you the one who troubles Israel?" Elijah could give a simple reply, but he wants to make the point emphatic that it is Ahab in his apostasy and idolatry that has troubled Israel; so he calls for a contest on Mount Carmel. The contest consists of offering sacrifice to the Baals and to the God of heaven. The answer will come in the form of fire. The God who will send fire from heaven to burn up the sacrifice will be the true God.

Ahab and his apostates offered their sacrifice to Baal and shouted, "O Baal, hear us. O Baal hear us." The record says, "Baal did not answer them a word." They shouted, danced around the altar and cried all day, and Elijah mocked by then telling them to shout louder and louder. "Maybe," he said, "your god is asleep, or away on a mission, or something is wrong with him." The more they called without an answer, the more frenzied they became until they even cut themselves. But at the end of the day it was the same. Baal did not answer. He could not answer. Then Elijah ordered the people to come near to him, and he put his sacrifice upon the altar built for the purpose. Then he prayed to the God of Abraham and said, "O Lord answer me, answer me so these people will know that you, O Lord, are God, and that you are turning their hearts back again." Immediately the fire came down from heaven and burned up the sacrifice. And the people fell prostrate and cried out, "The Lord, He is God! The Lord – He is God!" At this point Elijah commanded the people to seize the prophets of Baal, and he brought them down to the Kidron Valley and slaughtered them.

Then Elijah told Ahab and the people to go home quickly for it was going to rain (1 Kings 18).

Two points are made with emphasis: (1) That the Eternal speaks to His creatures on the earth. Those who hear are those who are willing to listen to Him. (2) That idols cannot speak, and no amount of sounds can wake them up. As the Psalmist puts it:

> They have mouths, but cannot speak, eyes, but they cannot see; they have ears, but they cannot hear; noses, but they cannot smell, they have hands, but they cannot feel; feet, but they cannot walk; nor can they utter a sound with their throats. Those who make them will be like them, and so will all who trust in them" (Psa 115:5-8).

On this latter point I make the further comment that corresponds with Scripture, namely, that those who consult idols (Isa 19:1) or pray to those that cannot save (Isa 45:20), will be dismayed (Jer 50:2), led astray (1 Cor 12:2), and thus be brought to shame (Isa 44:9). One should not conclude this comment without taking note of Isaiah, who speaks of the pathetic condition of the idolater who seeks to enter into a relationship with a thing that is so mute. It is a scrap of wood, half a piece of timber and half a god, which the idolater is not content only to fashion. Having fashioned it, he falls down and worships it. Hear the mockings of Isaiah when he states that:

The blacksmith takes a tool and works with it in the coals; he shapes an idol with hammers, he forges it with the might of his arm. He gets hungry and loses his strength; he drinks no water and grows faint. The carpenter measures with a line and makes an outline with a marker; he roughs it out with chisels and marks it with compasses. He shapes in the form of man, of man in all his glory, that it may dwell in a shrine. He cuts down cedars, or perhaps took a cypress or oak. He let it grow of the trees of the forest, or planted a pine, and the rain made it grow. It is man's fuel for burning; some of it he takes and warms himself, he kindles a fire and bakes bread. But he also fashions a god and worships it; he makes an idol and worships it. Half of the wood he burns in the fire; over it he prepares his meal, he roasts his meat and eats his fill. He also warms himself and says "Ah! I am warm; I see the fire." From the rest he makes a god, his idol; he bows down to it and worships. He prays to it and says, "Save me you are my god." They know nothing, they understand nothing; their eyes are plastered over so they cannot see, and their minds closed so they cannot understand. No one stops to think, no one has the knowledge to say, "Half of it I used for fuel; I even baked bread over its coals, I roasted meat and ate. Shall I make a detestable from what is left? Shall I bow down to a block of wood?" He feeds on ashes, a deluded misleads him; he cannot save himself, or say, "Is not this thing in my right hand a lie?" (Isaiah 44:12-20).

In effect, when idolaters cannot hear a word from their idols they enter into anxiety and total despair. They create more and more idols hoping to hear a word from them. In ancient times, as in ours, the noise that is made by idol worshippers in the search for a language by which they might dialogue is of profound interest. They even mechanize the lips of these gods so that they might seem to speak, though if they speak their words are but a parody. Yet the idolater is willing to accept any word, even a demonic word. The uncontrolled noises of some religious communities and the noises of the stadiums and the sounds of the discos may be symptoms of the secular quest to hear a word from the idols of culture. However, idols do not speak a divine word: they only lead us into falsehoods. Wherever there is a word from divine word, it is God speaking above the din of noise. In the midst of our chaos, He has issued His creative word. He commands with His word. He rules with His word. He relates with his word. And he judges by His word. God is the God who speaks. He speaks to us every day. He speaks in every circumstance of our lives. He might speak in a loud voice or in a small voice (1Kings 19:12). If only we will take the time to listen we are assured that we will hear Him.

In confrontation with God's silence

If God is the God who speaks, it remains a curious fact when God is silent. And the Scripture is clear that the Eternal cannot only speak but he can also be silent. While some statements say explicitly that God does not only speak but also that He can be silent, other Scriptures speak of his speech and silence in implicit ways. But the silence is different from the dumbness of the idols. God is not muzzled (Gk. *Ephimosen*) or voiceless (Gk. *aphonos*). He can speak (*dabar*) and he can be silent (*dumh*). His silence is very much connected with His nature. It speaks of Him as the Righteous Judge (the *Tzaddik* Heb.), as the One who is in full control of himself. He is right, straight, and righteous, in dispensing justice and is never wrong.[85] Chain Potok takes note of the *tzaddikim* (or righteous) leaders among the Hasidim Jewish sect who were supposed to be great teachers of the Law. Some persons believed them to be so holy that anything they touched became holy. Potok also notes that though some of these tzaddikims "were out and out frauds" who exploited their people terribly, in the major, they practiced righteous meditation in the Law and did much of their work in silence. They lived in silence and led their worship experiences with so much silence that one could feel the silence. The upright tzaddikims were most conscious that they were in the presence of God.[86]

In taking note of how God as the great *Tzaddik* acts in silence, I give attention to the creation, the flood, the covenant with Abraham, Sinai, the story of Saul, Elijah at Horeb, the story of Job, the silence at the cross, and the silence in the book of Revelation.

---

[85] See William Wilson on the idea concerning God, the "Righteous One" in Wilson's Old Testament Word Studies, (McLean, VA.: MacDonald Publishing Co).

[86] Chain Potok (1967), The Chosen (New York: Ballantine Books).

God's silence in the Creation

There is general agreement among theologians that the word of creation came from the silence of God, that is, out of nothingness. John says, "In the beginning was the Word, the Word was with God and the Word was God. All things were made by Him and nothing was made without him" (Jn 1:1,2). When God spoke His creative word, things happened. Then He was silent after he said, "Behold it is good," or "very good." In effect, the creation story is a rhythm of speech and silence. Some philosophical persons have seen in the creation story silence covering God's making of time and space. These are categories without sound, over against which stand the movements and sounds of nature.[87] There was in the creation a grand display of God's design without speech or language or voice (Psa 19:2-4). The Seventh-day Sabbath was like a silence pause in God's creative process. God ceased from all His SPOKEN works, and like the conductor of an orchestra, He anticipates a new phase. It is time to celebrate the music and move on.

Silence for Noah

In Genesis 7:4 we find that God declared to Noah that after seven days He was going to send the rain for forty days and nights. Noah built an ark according to the divine instruction, and when Noah and his family entered the ark, the hand of God closed its door. A friend with whom I dialogued as I was thinking through the meaning of God's action here suggested that this closing of the ark signaled that God had met in the divine Council and had determined judgment on the earth against a rebellious humanity.[88]

---

[87] Andre Neher (1981), The Exile of the Word: From the Silence of the Bible to the Silence of Auschwitz (Philadelphia: The Jewish Publication Society of America), 73

[88] Thanks to my Pastor Jose Luna for dialoging with me on the meaning of the silence which Noah experienced for seven days.

Within the first seven days that Noah and his family went into the ark, there was "silence in heaven." There was no rain. God, as it were, did not speak. There was judgment. The people outside were triumphant with scourging and mocking, and had no sense of their own doom. Silently and imperceptibly the clouds of rain were forming, and soon "the floods came and swept them all away" (Matt 24:38). In His Olivet discourse on the Last Judgment, Jesus said, "As it was in the days of Noah, so shall also the coming of the Son of Man be" (Matt 24:39).[89] The warnings of judgment are given, but many persons refuse to listen and are thus caught unawares.

Not to be forgotten concerning the seven days of silence that confronted Noah and his family is the fact that this was a test of their faith. We might imagine what it must have been for them. No cloud, no thunder, no rain, no voice, only the promise, this was a time when their anxiety might have led them to break their faith, but they held fast. In seven days the cloud, the thunder, the rain and the voice came. The seven days were quite symbolic, as an indication of how God brings judgment upon His people. In the journeying of Israel from Egypt, when Miriam sinned against Moses, she was shut out of the camp for seven days. The whole camp abode in Hazeroth and awaited her return. Not until she was shut out from the camp did the favor of God rest upon the tabernacle again (cf. Num 12:15ff).[90] In effect, one of the most important issues that is to be confronted in silence is judgment.

God's silence in establishing his covenant with Abraham

We also find a great display of the divine silence in the covenant test of Abraham. In the story, which is developed in Genesis 22, the silence is not only that of Abraham, but also that of

---

[89] Ellen White (copyright 1939), Great Controversy (Mountain View Calif.: Pacific Press), 491.
[90] Ellen White (copyright 1958), Patriarchs and Prophets (Mountain View Calif.: Pacific Press), 343

God. When Abraham was called to the land of Moriah, to offer Isaac as a sacrifice, Abraham did not tell Sarah, and even as he traveled along the way in the company of Eliezer and Isaac, he was steeped in silence and solitude. Soren Kierkegaard, who has been accepted as the most penetrating commentator on the story, says that what was most terrifying for Abraham in the story was the collision between God's command and God's command.[91] Abraham knew that God had commanded against one human being killing another by stating that "Whoever sheds the blood of a human by a human shall that person's blood be shed; for in his own image God made humankind" (cf. Gen 9:6). Now when he confronted the command, "Take your son, your only son Isaac, whom you love, and go to the land of Moriah and offer him there on one of the mountains that I will show you"(Gen 22:2), he had to wonder if there was a contradiction in God's command. As friend of God, Abraham knew God's voice and was willing to obey. But along the road to Moriah Abraham did not hear a further word from God. Kierkegaard suggests suspension of all reason and speculation when he says that the faith of Abraham never turns to a single question. Kierdegaard insinuates some questions that he offers to other persons, but not to Abraham, "the hero of faith." He rightly indicates that the act of offering Isaac was more difficult than if Abraham had no faith. He thinks that if he had no faith, he would have found it a simple act to murder Isaac, like other persons in his social context. But he had faith, and, though he shared a depth of anxiety and pain as any father would, yet he did not question, he only obeyed. But Kierkegaard seems to suggest a question when he states that Abraham at least wondered whether, if he had misunderstood God, where he would turn.[92] The points at issue for us: note first that as Abraham walked the way to Moriah and confronted the silence of God, it must have been as difficult

---

[91] Soren Kierkegaard (1983), Fear and Trembling, edited and translated by Howard V. Hong and Edna Hong, (Princeton, New Jersey: Princeton Univ. Press), 248.
[92] Ibid., 250.

for him as it is for any person of faith who faces the silence of God. The second issue is that when God gives a command, He does not need to recite that word again and again. God's command is final. His command is His first and last word.

God's silence at Sinai

From the story of Abraham we make a long jump to the story of the divine silence at Sinai. The preface to the Ten Commandments says:

> Israel encamped in front of the mountain . . . . Moses went up to the Elohim. And Yahweh called him from the mountain and said, this is what you shall say to the house of Jacob and reveal to the sons of Israel. You yourselves have seen what I have done to the Egyptians and how I carried you on the wings of eagles and brought you to myself. And now if you will obey my voice and keep my covenant, you will be for me, out of all the peoples, a special treasure, for the whole earth is mine. And you, yourselves, you will be for me a priestly realm and a holy nation. These are the words that you will speak to the sons of Israel" (Ex 19:1-6.).

After communing with God, Moses left the mountain and then spoke to the people telling them to consecrate themselves for their meeting with God on the third day. There were thunders and flashes of lightning, and a heavy cloud upon the mountain (19:16). Thus the people knew that God was on the mountain. They could hear his voice in the thunder roar and see him in the cloud of smoke. They knew that the God of Israel was different from the gods of Egypt. He could speak. The priest then blew the shophar with strength, and Moses spoke, and God answered him from the thunder (19:19). The Lord gave Moses further instructions for the people and asked him to go down and get Aaron. Moses told the people what God said for the preparation, and then God spoke the ten words - - the Ten Commandments.

When the people saw the thunder and the lightening and heard the trumpet and saw smoke, they trembled with fear. They stayed at a distance and said to Moses, "Speak to us yourself and we will listen. But do not have God speak to us or we will die" (20:19).

Having warned the people that what they were seeing and hearing was a test from God, Moses went up into the thick darkness and for the next forty days received the instructions of God. There is much evidence that the thunder stopped as Moses received the further words. The God of Sinai was different from the gods of the Egyptians. God can speak and God can be silent.

We are not told explicitly when the thunder stopped, but it is evident that this occurred while the subsidiary laws were being given to Moses. For one thing, later in the narrative (Exodus 32) we are told that when the people saw that Moses had taken so long to come down from the mountain, they gathered around Aaron and demanded that he make for them the Golden Calf. My comment is that this could be expected, for when a people stops hearing the divine voice, they often become anxious, lose faith and turn to idolatry. This is not always the case, but when human rebellion is confronting that silence there is often a turning to idolatry.

Saul the prophet without a word from God

One of the challenging stories of Scripture that brings out the above point is told in the 28th chapter of 1 Samuel. At the beginning of his kingship it was proclaimed that Saul was also among the prophets (1 Sam 9). A little later in his kingship he consulted the Urim (that is the stone upon the breastplate of the priest) but did not hear from God (1 Sam 14:37), so he assumed that someone in his camp was guilty (vv. 38-39). The case, as he found it, was against Jonathan. Of course, the transgression of Jonathan was not like the sin of Saul in exposing the soldiers to hunger and death. Only with the people's intervention was

Jonathan spared. Saul continued in his sinful ways, and at the end of his days he once again consulted the *Urim* but did not hear from God. With the rebuking words of the prophet Samuel still ringing in his ears, telling him that God had rejected him, he went to the witch of Endor and consulted with the apparition. Since Saul was cut off from God and his intermediaries, he turned to the other side – tragic magic and its idols.[93] He knew that in all of his pretensions, the Divine would not be there with him.

Silence at Horeb

In passing from the story of Carmel where Elijah invoked God to speak his word through the fire, we come to the contrasting story of Elijah's meeting with God at Horeb. Here is a rather intense revelation of the divine. First, God spoke to Elijah, asking him what he was doing there in the cave on the mountain. Then He advised Elijah to get to the top of the mountain to be in the presence of the Lord; for the Lord was about to pass by:

> Then a great and powerful wind tore the mountains apart and shattered the rocks before the Lord, but the Lord was not in the wind. After the wind there was an earthquake, but the Lord was not in the earthquake, after the earthquake came a fire, but the Lord was not in the fire. And after the fire came a sound of sheer silence. When Elijah heard it, he wrapped his face in his mantle and went out and stood at the entrance of the cave. Then there came a voice to him and said, "What are you doing here Elijah?" (1 Kings 19:9lp-13fp).

For Andre Neher, perhaps there is no passage in the Bible which puts the God who speaks to the test more than 1 Kings 19:11-14. What is seen is how the futility of the divine speech is confronted in the same context as its efficaciousness. Thus the word is transposed into silence on the same day that it seemed to

---

[93] Ibid., 73, 74

have established the truth of God.[94] That means that God does not only speak powerfully, but God is manifested in a voice of stillness. The point is that God does not only speak (Heb. *qol*); God can be silent (Heb. *dumh*). For Jerome T Walsh, silence puts Yahweh beyond all natural phenomena but also beyond all human ability to comprehend Him.[95] In distinction to the other gods who are only to be found in nature, God is over nature. He can stand silent.

Silence in the book of Job

The same point is made in the book of Job where the silence of God is most difficult for humanity to understand (Job 4:12-17). But it is not only that God's silence is so challenging but also that Satan uses the occasion to malign the character of God. The story is introduced with God and Satan in intense dialogue. Satan is not satisfied just to argue with God; he really wishes to challenge the justice of God by using Job as his foil. But as the story develops, we are presented with the longest statement in Scripture of God's silence, for God does not seek at every stage to speak on God's behalf. When God becomes silent, humanity takes over and fills the void with speech. Willful humanity, represented in the persons of Job's wife and Job's friends, say "everything." They argue that God does not allow righteous people to suffer. They say that human beings cannot be pure before their Maker. They also declare that God does not put His trust in mortals or angels. Thus Andre Neher says that so much rhetoric has been expended between chapters 3 and 37 that it left Job with the temptation to think that he was hearing the voice of God through the voices of his friends. When the divine voice is finally heard, Job is subjected to a contrary temptation, that of thinking that he is

---

[94] Ibid., 84.
[95] Jerome T. Walsh (1996), Berit Olam: Studies in Hebrew Narrative and Poetry (Collegeville, MN: The Liturgical Press), 276.

hearing the voice of men through the voice of God. Job has had to swim across the ocean of human words, which mimic the voice of God. This Neher calls "the silence of conspiracy," when Satan seeks to cut off the voice of God from us.[96] This is what Satan does; he cuts off the voice of the divine so that he can speak to us and bring us into slavery to himself.

Silence at the cross

A further example of God's silence, which we would be found remiss if we should fail to make mention, is the silence of the Cross. This silence occurred just before the death of Jesus. When the entire burden of sin was upon Him, He listened for the same voice that He had heard at His baptism and on the mount of transfiguration to say, "This is my Son, my beloved," but He heard no voice. He thus cried out, "My God! My God! Why have you forsaken me?" Helmut Theilike reflects upon this and says that the cross was God's greatest silence.

The power of darkness was allowed to make its final bid against the Son of God. Then the demons were unleashed and the most dreadful passions since the fall of Adam were given free reign. And God had nothing to say. There was simply the cry of the Dying asking the silence why God had forsaken him. God was still silent even when the dumb nature began to speak in eloquent gesture and the sun withdrew its light. The stars cried out and God was silent.[97]

It is a great point of interest for me that Jesus experienced this palpable silence. Ellen White says that there was silence in heaven; no harp was touched. As the angels saw their Lord

---

[96] Andre Neher (1981), The Exile of the Word: From the Silence of the Bible to the Silence of Auschwitz (Philadelphia: The Jewish Publications Society of America), 32.

[97] Helmut Theilike (1962), The Silence of God (Grand Rapids, MI: Wm. B. Eerdmans), 14.

enclosed by legions of satanic forces, His human nature weighed down with a shuddering, mysterious dread. Yet for a moment heaven was silent.[98] "The enemies of Jesus vented their rage upon Him as He hung upon the cross. Priests, rulers, and scribes joined with the mob in mocking the dying Savior. At the baptism and at the transfiguration the voice of God had been heard proclaiming Christ as His Son. Again, just before Christ's betrayal, the Father had spoken, witnessing to His divinity. But now the voice from heaven was silent. No testimony to His divinity. But now the voice from heaven was silent. No testimony in Christ's favor was heard. Alone He suffered abuse and mockery from wicked men."[99] In the silence Christ felt abandoned as we feel abandonment, but His was total abandonment. Although He felt the abandonment He did not turn to humanity for comfort, nor did He whine and complain, as is often the case with us. He cried to His Father, and asked, "My God! My God! Why have you abandoned me?" for He knew that only His Father had an answer to deal with the silence of sin's abandonment. Theilike says that even while God did not answer Jesus a word or syllable, God made this hour a great turning point by rending the veil of the temple and laying his heart bare with all its wounds. When it was thought for the weekend that Jesus was trapped in the silence of death, He came forth from the grave on Sunday morning with a voice more clear than that with which He had spoken on Friday. In the trial on Friday Jesus, the Divine Exegete, said very little. What God wanted to say to humanity was already said.[100] Jesus could be still as the Father was still. But the silence did not mean that all was over.

---

[98] Ellen White (1999 compilation), Christ Triumphant (Hagerstown, MD: Review & Herald), 265

[99] Ibid., 278.

[100] Helmut Theilike (1962), The Silence of God (Grand Rapids, MI: Wm. B. Eerdmans), 14.

Silence at the end

In the New Testament and in the Epistles nothing more is said of the silence of God at the cross, but after the record of the great enthronement of Christ noted in Revelation 4, and the opening of the seals reflected on in Revelation 5-7, we confront the remarkable silence that seems to be the prelude to the end. The questions, which have been persistent for us, are; "What is this final moment of silence?" "Why is there silence instead of speech?" "Is it that God has withdrawn from humanity as He seems to have done while Christ was hanging there on the cross?" "Is it that the world is to confront another moment of judgment as it did while Christ was hanging there on the cross?" "Is it that God is about to call into being conditions of life as He did when He first created the world out of silence?" "Is it that God is about to bring to a close the great cosmic conflict and name Himself as the true God as he did in microcosmic form upon mount Carmel with Elijah and the prophets of Baal?" "Is it that God is withdrawing Himself for yet a little while, as He did in mercy while tolerating the arrogance of the Satanic accusation as it happened in the story of Job?"

We mentioned earlier in this discussion that in the dramatic story of Job, God is silent while Satan accuses the justice of God and while the friends of Job, who think themselves righteous, speak superfluously for God. The God who once spoke eloquently of His righteousness in the prologue of Job and the God who speaks in the end refuses throughout the drama to say a single word. When at the end God speaks, He asks Job how well he understood the story of creation and the providences of God. Job was overwhelmed; he could hardly speak. He, more than his friends, came to understand the righteousness and the providences of God. Job came to see that there was a controversy in the world and that the children of God often got caught up in the battles. When God spoke, Job therefore grasped himself and answered in a few short words (Job 40:3-5). Only words of praise for the divine justice was all Job could offer.

We shall return to the above questions in a following discussion. What seems to be clear here is that the God who speaks and acts and stands is a God who can sit in the silence of a judge in a judgment hall and the silence of an accused who takes "the Fifth." God is not a criminal and needs not answer for himself, but he has chosen in His freedom to answer, for in His answer is the salvation of humanity. God has the first word and the last word, but God can be silent. He sometimes seems to be silent to allow for dialogue with us humans. But at other times He is silent in confrontation with us. When Satan and humanity try to accuse God of injustice, God knows who is in the right. God does not need to defend himself with eloquent speech. His defense is often in silence. Speech, some persons will say, led God to the cross. But I would argue, as Isaiah (cf. Isa 53) does, that it was not so much speech but silence. It was not just Christ's words, but also His silence that contradicted those who crucified Him. "He was oppressed, and he was afflicted, yet he did not open his mouth; like a lamb that is led to the slaughter, and like a sheep that before its shearer is silent, so he did not open his mouth" (Isa 53: 7).

Of a truth, God will not do wickedly,
And the Almighty will not pervert justice.
When he is quiet, who can condemn?
When he hides his face, who can behold him, whether it be a nation or an individual? (Job 34:12,29).

IV

SILENCE IN THE COSMIC COURTROOM

No word is God's last word

We concluded our last discussion with the assertion that God not only has the first word but also the last word. We open this discussion with the assertion of Abraham Heschel that "No word is God's last word."[101] This declaration also agrees with what we said in our previous discussion: that God does not always speak. He speaks because He wills and does not speak when He wills. Humans cannot reduce God to silence, nor can they force God to speak. Heschel speaks of the silence of God distancing Himself from us, as God remaining invisible to us, as God dwelling in darkness. At those times when the prophets' voices were not heard, and those times when the prophets could not hear the Lord, they spoke of the silence of God.[102] In reality God did withdraw from Israel (Hosea 5:6), and at various times He did not communicate with the prophets (Lam 2:9). He did this as an act of judgment against His apostate people. When God comes to judgment he begins with his people.

Bible historians speak of the times of Israel's captivity and the time of the Intertestamental period of four hundred years (from Malachi to John the Baptist) when there were no prophets' words to Israel as times of Israel's judgment. When the covenanted people failed to listen to God, no new prophetic word was sent to them. For Amos such a time was to come.

---

[101] Abraham J. Heschel (1962), **The Prophet** (New York: Harper & Row) 193.
[102] Ibid., 193.

> Behold the days are coming, says the Lord, when I will send a famine on the land; not a famine for bread, nor a thirst for water, but of hearing the words of the Lord. They shall wander from sea to sea, and from north to east; they shall run to and fro, to seek the word of the Lord, but they shall not find it (Amos 8: 11-12).

The absence of God from His temple

Another way in which God brought judgment to His people was to withdraw from his temple. The temple, in Jewish tradition and many other ancient traditions, was the scene of judgment. The priests were not only religious in their functions but also civil in their work of judgment. Their work in worship was a work of judgment. It was thus often carried on in solemn silence. I have reviewed, in the introductory chapter, how silence functioned in the inner sanctuary of Jewish worship experience, but a brief reminder is appropriate here. It states that the sounds of the outer court were not offered in the inner temple where the priest atoned for the repentant people. Outside of the priestly confessional prayer, the activity of the priest was carried on in "holy silence." The prayers of the people, the tuneful melodies, the hymns and the tumultuous folk cult were rendered in the court. The temple was built with circles of sound and silence distinct from one another. In the inner temple the silence was often so complete that it seemed that not a single person was present.[103] By the use of analogy one can try to imagine that the service of worship and the judgment that is taking place in the heavenly temple also involve sounds and silence. There are the happy songs for the divine work of creation and redemption (cf. Rev 4, 5). There are messages of warning to all mortals who are to appear at the judgment that is taking place (Rev 6). There is also a reminder to the guardian angels for the marking of the true people of God (Rev 7); all of this

---

[103] Israel Knohl, "Between Voice and Silence: The Relationship Between Prayer and Temple Cult," Journal of Biblical Literature, 115/1 (1996): 17-30.

is followed by silence or the silent service of judgment (Rev 8:1). What the prophet Jeremiah says concerning this subject is insightful: "I will hide my face from the city because of all its wickedness" (Jer. 33:5).

In the extensive vision of the divine judgment against the Jerusalem temple prophet Ezekiel gives us clear understanding of the dynamic movement between the divine voice and His silence. In chapters 1-7 the prophet sees God coming to His temple to begin a work of judgment against his people who have brought every work of corruption into the temple. In the eighth chapter the prophet then says that he was transported to the temple in order to see the departing glory of the Lord. The reason for the departing glory is spelled out in detail. He is taken to the north gate and sees "the idol of jealousy." Then he is shown "more detestable things." Through a hole in the outer wall, which he is invited to dig, he sees all kinds of idolatrous pictures scrawled on the inner walls. This creates a deep hurt for the prophet, for he sees seventy of the elders of Israel with censers in their hands, standing in the darkness, each before one of the idolatrous pictures. They are burning their incense to their idols, thinking or saying to themselves "the Lord does not see us." When he is transported to another gate of the temple, he sees women "sitting there, mourning for Tammuz," the ancient Akkadian deity professed to be the husband and brother of Ishtar.[104] From the north gate he is taken to the inner court of the house of the Lord, and there, in the entrance of the temple, between the portico and the altar, he sees twenty-five men with their backs toward the temple of the Lord, and their faces turned toward the east. They are doing obeisance to the sun. And there is more: when he is taken outside of the temple again, he sees a scene of total injustice and violence plaguing the land.

Chapter nine of Ezekiel records the judgment of God being carried forward against the idolatry, injustice and violence of the

---

[104] For a discussion on Tammuz see Frank Gaebelein, general editor (1986), The Expositor's Bible Commentary, Volume 6 (Isaiah-Ezekiel) (Grand Rapids, MI: Zondervan) 783-784.

people. The executioners of the city, who are elected by divine authority, are invited to bring their weapons and kill. Before the destruction takes place, the Lord requests an agent of mercy who carries a writing case at his side to go throughout the city of Jerusalem and put a mark on the foreheads of those who lament over all the detestable things that are done in the land. Once the mark is given, God issues a further command to the executioners, namely to "Follow through the city and kill, without showing pity or compassion. Slaughter old men, young men and maidens, women and children, but do not touch anyone who has the mark. Begin at my sanctuary" (9:5-6). The executioners begin with the elders that are in front of the temple. The further command is to defile the house and fill the temple courts with the slain. This scene of bloodshed carries a profound impact on the prophet, who intercedes with the Lord by asking, "Lord, God, are you going to destroy all of the remnant of Israel as you pour out your wrath upon Jerusalem?" (9:8). The Lord answers that "The guilt of the House of Israel and Judah has become so great; the land is full of bloodshed and perversity because the dwellers have thought that the Lord has forsaken the land and does not see." In effect, God assures the prophet that the divine command of judgment has to be carried to its completion.

In Chapters 10 and 11, there is an extension of the vision concerning the reasons for the judgment. And there is greater emphasis on the movement of the glory of God from the temple. The scene picks up in the Most Holy Place where the cherubims are seen over the Ark of the Covenant and the Seat of the Presence (cf. Ex 25:18-20), and the gradual movement of God already identified in chapter 9:3 progresses. In 10:4 the glory, which leaves the Most Holy Place, moves to the temple entrance and beyond. An outline of the departure is interesting:

1. The glory of the Lord fills the inner court (10:3)
2. The glory of the Lord departs from the inner court to the threshold (10:4)

3. The glory of the Lord moves from the threshold and stops above the cherubim in the outer court (10:18)
4. The glory of God moves from the outer court to the east gate of the House of the Lord (10:19)
5. The glory of God moves from the east gate to the Mount of Olives (11:23).

During the progressive movement of the divine glory, the judgment of God is executed against twenty-five of the civic leaders who are gathered at the gate in their counsel of wickedness. They have given the people false counsel, planned evil things, practiced oppression and murder against the poor, and told others to build houses at a time when God has been announcing the destruction of Jerusalem by the Babylonians. In chapter 11, as more of the perversion of the leaders is seen, Ezekiel prophesies to the leaders that their actions are not hidden from God's omniscience. God knows exactly what they are thinking, saying, and doing (v. 5).[105] The prophet thus informs the leaders that they and their followers will be brought outside the "pot" of Jerusalem and struck down with the sword of foreigners (11:8-11). When the judgment is completed against them, there is the prospect of redemption for those who practice the principles of the covenant. The Lord's promise to Ezekiel is that He will gather the remnant and fill them with his Spirit.

> "I will give them one heart and put a new spirit within them; I will remove the heart of stone from their flesh and give them a heart of flesh, so that they may follow up my statutes and keep my ordinances and obey them. Then they shall be my people and I will be their God. But as for those whose hearts go after their detestable things and their abominations, I will bring their deeds upon their own heads says the Lord." (11:19-21)

After God has given to Ezekiel encouragement concerning the future restoration of the remnant of Judah and the restoration of

---

[105] Frank Gaebelein, general editor (1986), <u>The Expositor's Bible Commentary</u>, Volume 6 (Isaiah-Ezekiel) (Grand Rapids, MI: Zondervan) 791.

the land, the glory of the Lord departs east from Jerusalem to the Mount of Olives (11:22-23). Gaebelein notes that after this departure, the presence of the Lord among the Israelites is depicted as being removed until Ezekiel 43:1-4. The reality of the judgment is thus certain.[106] Briefly connecting this review to the understanding from Jeremiah makes us aware that for three and a half years the presence tarried on the Mount of Olives proclaiming three times daily that the sons of the wayward Israel should return (Jer 3:22). For a while God turns His back upon the scene; He does not speak. But then in mercy He calls for the repentance of His people as in the end He will call for the destruction of the wicked.

A number of issues are generated from the review of the extended vision of the progressive departure of the divine glory from the temple and the consequent judgment upon Israel. The first issue is that the portrayal is consistent with the withdrawal of the divine glory at other times when Israel rebelled against God and His prophetic word of warning was neglected. In 1 Samuel 4, for example, the departure is memorialized by the name of Eli's grandson, "Ichabod" (v. 21), which means "inglorious."[107] In Deuteronomy 31:17 and Hosea 9:12 it was declared that God's presence would depart if the people strayed from God's ways.[108] After the building of the golden calf, recorded in Exodus 32, and 33, God instructs Moses that Israel might "Go up to the land flowing with milk and honey; but, I will not go up among you, or I would consume you on the way, for you are a stiff-necked people" (v. 3). Moses is also told to take the tent of meeting and pitch it far from the camp, so that any one who sought the Lord would have to go out to the tent. In Amos no explicit statement of the Lord's departure is made. However, in the context of Israel's apostasy and the divine declaration of judgment, the prophet sees the Lord standing beside a wall built with a plumbline, measuring the city.

---

[106] Ibid., 794.
[107] Ibid., 790.
[108] Ibid., 790.

The wall is evidently outside of the temple, and from it God announces the destruction of the high places, the sanctuaries of Israel and the desolation of the temple itself (Amos 7, 8). Later the prophet sees God standing beside the altar instructing His agents to strike the capitals until the thresholds shake and the heads of all the people are shattered. The judgment is to be made complete with the devastation of all evil and the restoration of the remnant of the covenant.

Fig 4:1

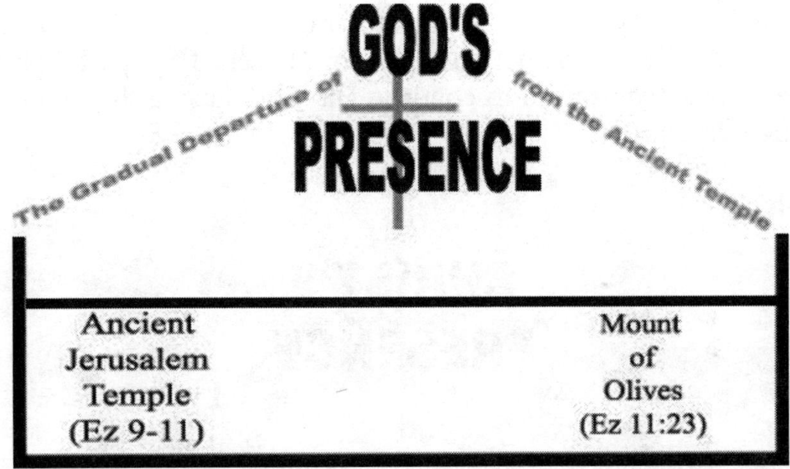

The writings of the other prophets can be searched for the history of the departure of the divine glory from the temple. But a review would not be complete if no mention were made of the words of Jesus as recorded by Matthew concerning the corruption of the Jewish religion and God's departure from the temple. For a last time, Jesus stood in the temple precinct condemning the hypocrisy of the religious leaders. They had killed the prophets, the sages and other teachers of the law. Jesus, therefore, says:

> "Jerusalem, Jerusalem, the city that kills the prophets and stones those who are sent to it! How often have I desired to gather your children together as a hen gathers her brood

> under her wings, and you were not willing! See your house is left to you desolate. For I tell you, you will not see me again until you say, Blessed is the one who comes in the name of the Lord!" (23: 37-39).

As He departed, He walked slowly, even stopping in the outer court for a conversation with the Greeks who came to inquire if He were the Christ. He struggled to leave, with the urgent understanding that His work in the temple was finished. He thus summoned His disciples and left; not as one defeated and forced from the presence of His adversaries, but as one whose work was accomplished. "He retired as a victor from the contest."[109] But here His departure was not absolute, for He sent His Spirit to be His earthly Advocate and to continue His work among the nations (Lk 24:49; Acts 2:1).

Fig 4:2

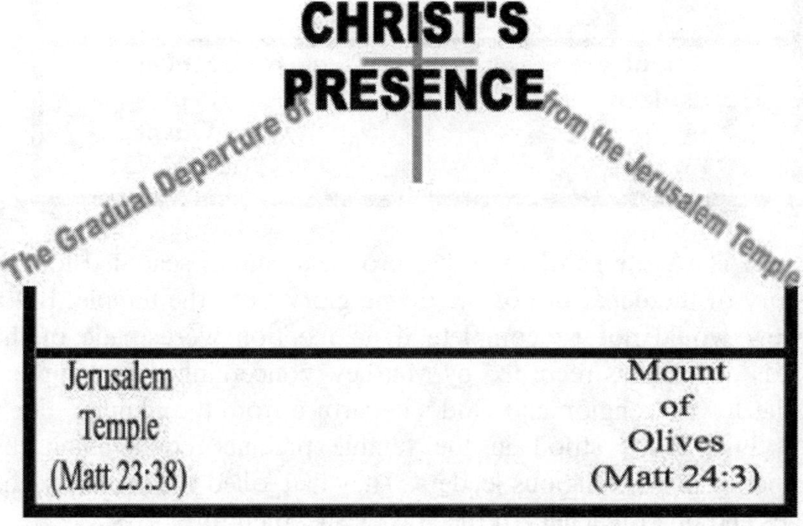

---

[109] Ellen White (1940 edition), Desire of Ages (Mountain View, Calif.: Pacific Press Publishing Assoc.), 640.

The second notable issue is that when God leaves the heavenly sanctuary humanity is confronted with the grammar of divine silence. In such a context Daniel prays, "Now therefore, O our God, listen to the prayer of your servant and to his supplication, and for your sake, Lord, let your face shine upon your desolate sanctuary" (9:17). Responding to the prayer of Solomon during the dedication of Solomon's temple, God said, in Solomon's dream:

> "When I shut up the heaven so that there is no rain, or command the locust to devour the land, or send pestilence among the people. . . If my people who are called by my name will humble themselves and pray, seek my face, and turn from their wicked ways, then I will hear from heaven, and will forgive their sins and heal their land" (1 Chron 7:13,14).

Again, when Eli got old and his sons practiced their evil in the house of the Lord, the comment was made, "The word of the Lord was rare in those days, and visions were not widespread" (1 Sam 3:1). For Amos, of whom we spoke at the beginning of this chapter, the time is coming when there will be a famine for the word of God (Amos 8:11). Other parts of Scripture might be pursued to make the point that when God leaves His temple, or sanctuary, even the wicked pray but hear no word from God. No wonder they think that "There is no God" (Psa 10:4) or that there is no one to call them to account (10:13). We know what is true, for Job (from an earlier discussion) has informed us that it is not that God is absent but that God often refuses to participate in the discussions of foolish human beings (Job 4-37). In a brief return to contemplate the silence from the temple we note that which we picked up in Ezekiel's vision, namely, that what drives God away is the great abominations of His people (Ez 8:6). William Shea comments, "Yahweh's departure from His temple is not an arbitrary action carried out on His part; His people had driven Him from His own house."[110]

The third factor to which I wish to pay keen attention is the fact that one can take the passage from Ezekiel and fit it into the theme of silence and judgment as it is offered to us in the Apocalypse. While Ezekiel focuses on the divine judgment that took place from the Jerusalem temple, John, who uses Ezekiel's vision as a starting point focuses on the judgment that takes place in the sanctuary in heaven.[111] The judgment is in the same context of worship as in Ezekiel, and the dominant symbols set forth in his vision of the four living creatures encircling the throne of God, remain. It is not a redundant issue when the angel later in the book announces, "Fear God and give him glory, for the hour of his judgment has come; and worship him who made the heaven and the earth, the sea and the springs of water" (Rev 14:6). The point is that in His speech and silence in the sanctuary, God is in judgment. When He sits in the sanctuary with the host around His throne, one aspect of the judgment begins and is carried forward (cf. Dan 7:10, 26; Ez 9, 10; Rev 4-7). When He departs from the sanctuary (Ez 9-11; Rev 8:1), another aspect of the judgment begins (Ez 12-35; Rev 8:2-20:15).

Silence in the courtroom

Let us think of silence in the heavenly courtroom in terms of the contemporary courtroom experience. But we must first remind ourselves of what Thomas Finger says, namely, that the biblical concept of judgment is not to be limited to a courtroom scene in which sentences of punishment or reward are handed out.

---

[110] William Shea, (1981), "The Investigative Judgment of Judah, Ezekiel 1-10," Studies in
The Sanctuary and the Atonement, Biblical, Historical and Theological, eds. A. Wallenkampf and W. R. Lesher (Washington, D.C: Review and Herald), 283-291.

[111] R. Dean Davis (1992), The Heavenly Courtroom Judgment of Revelation 4-5 (Latham, MD: University Press of America).

That is to say, the legal characterization must not be taken as the "be all" and "end all" of matters.

> "Biblical trials . . . are not merely courtroom trials. They are historical struggles, historical conflicts, between forces of good and of evil. These forces might . . . sometimes confront each other in court. But their conflict is not resolved with the mere declaration of a verdict. It is resolved with the defeat of evil and the triumph of good."[112]

In our local courtrooms, clerks, counsels and court attendants often bustle about and consult together until the judge comes in and the order is given that the court trial is open. No more word is heard until the judge gives his/her opening statement as to what constitutes the proceedings of the day. The judge then reads the charges and the trial proceeds. Each trial constitutes a solemn moment, and both the judge and the accused are bound to keep silent. The judge keeps silent because the judge is not on trial. An attorney often speaks for an accused. Or, an accused might decide to "take the Fifth," if he/she does not wish to be implicated. Of course, there is something that is of interest about the accused. If the person is pressed and refuses to confess, the judge might charge such a person with defiance of the court. In which case the person goes to jail anyway. In the heavenly court trial the one who speaks on behalf of the accused is Christ. For those who confess their sins to Him, it is enough that He is their Heavenly Attorney. No one can take "the fifth" in heaven's court because God is a reader of each heart. Jesus illustrates this in the parable of the man without the wedding robe. When he was asked by the king, "Friend, how did you get in here without a wedding robe? He was speechless" (Matt 22:1-12). He likely took "the fifth." But in the heavenly court "the fifth" is nothing. Taking the

[112] Thomas Finger (1991), Christian Theology: An Eschatological Approach, Vol. I (Kitchener, Ontario: Herald Press), 145.

fifth only brings self-condemnation. This is why the king in the parable of the wedding commands the attendants, "Bind him hand and foot, and throw him into outer darkness, where there will be weeping and gnashing of teeth" (v. 13). As with the man without the wedding robe, so with the hypocrite (Lk 13:28), and the worthless slaves or servants (Matt 24:51; 25:30); God reads their hearts. "The Lord searches every mind and understands every plan and thought" (1 Chron 28:9). He is a "God who searches the heart," and He knows what is in the mind of the Spirit, because "the Spirit intercedes for the saints" (Rom 8:27). But the silence of the judge in the heavenly court can be sustained because no one can pass condemnation against the judge, nor against His saints. Before putting this whole paragraph into a systematic formulation, let us note the beautiful picture as Paul states it:

> What then are we to say about these things? If God is for us, who can be against us? He who did not withhold his own Son, but gave him up for all of us, will he not with him give us everything else? Who will bring any charge against God's elect? It is God who justifies. Who is it that condemns? It is Christ Jesus, who died, yes, who was raised, who sits at the right of God, who intercedes for us. Who will separate us from the love of Christ? Will hardship, or distress, or persecution, or famine, or nakedness, or peril, or sword? As it is written, 'For your sake we are being killed all day long; we are accounted as sheep to be slaughtered.' No, in all these things we are more than conquerors, through him who loved us. For I am convinced that neither death, nor life, nor angels, nor rulers, nor things present, nor things to come, nor powers, nor height, nor depth, nor anything else in all creation, will be able to separate us from the love of God in Christ Jesus the Lord (Rom 8:31-39).

In reference to the question "Who can bring a charge against God's elect?" one might expect an answer other than the one Paul gives. Someone might think, for example, that Satan can bring a charge. Satan is called "The Accuser of the saints" (Rev 12:10), and he does this most effectively when he seeks to frighten the saints with his loud noises. According to the prophet Zechariah, on one occasion Satan tried to bring an accusation, if not a charge against Joshua, the high priest, while Joshua was offering the sacrifice of confession at the altar. The accusation was that Joshua was there with a filthy garment of sin. He was therefore unworthy to offer the confession and could not be forgiven. But while Satan was laying his accusation, the angelic messenger ordered those standing around to take off the filthy garment (of sin) from Joshua and clothe him with a garment of righteousness (the righteousness of God). Satan has no further argument. God simply says that he will send the Branch, His servant, to remove the sin of Israel in a single day and take away the reproach (Zech 3). This forms the backdrop of what Paul is stating when he says that no one can bring a (single) charge against those whom God has declared justified (Rom 8:1).

When God sits in judgment, Satan brings his accusations against the saints; but because of the sacrifice of Christ, Satan stands dumb, disobedient human beings are dumb, and the saints need not say anything for themselves. Indeed, they cannot, for only Christ as their Advocate can speak for them (Rom 8:33). The Apostle John reminds us that we have an Advocate with the Father (1Jn 2:1). He also makes mention of the Holy Spirit as our advocate (Jn 14:6). Job also said that he knew that his Advocate (Hebrew, *Goel*, also translated, Referee, Redeemer) lives, and that in the end He will stand upon the earth or upon his grave (Job 19:25). Job well understood that Satan, the Accuser of the brethren, would seek to fight against God and even try to hold the saints of God in their graves, with the charge that they cannot be forgiven of all their sins. But a perfect God as the judge does not need to speak to Satan or anyone of His own righteousness. God is in the right. He is righteous. He does not need to make a case for His justice. His case has been made already at the cross. And even there He did not need to speak. As a phrase from the Servant passage in Isaiah declares, "He did not open His mouth" (Isa 53:7). He seemed powerless, but so is the mystery of the divine strength (1 Cor 1:21-27). In His trial Jesus could speak for Himself, but much emphasis is laid on the fact that He was silent. During the act of crucifixion He could also speak for Himself, but He was silent. He could speak as God can speak for Himself, but He did not say "a mumbling word." His silence was His word of judgment upon His crucifiers.

Some persons might contend that the following reflection which I took from an internet seems commonplace. But I think it emphasizes the point concerning the right of the divine to be silent. It says:

> At the end of time, billions of people were scattered on a great plain before God. They shrank back from the brilliant light before them. But some groups near the front talked, not with cringing shame, but with belligerence. "Can God judge us? How can he know about suffering?" snapped a pert young brunette, who ripped open a sleeve to reveal a tattooed number from a Nazi concentration camp. 'With terror.... Beatings... torture...death!
>
> In another group a negro boy lowered his collar. "What about this?" He demanded, shaggily, Rope burn. Lynched for no crime but being black!
>
> In another crowd, a pregnant schoolgirl with sullen eyes asks, "Why should I suffer? It wasn't my fault."
>
> Far out across the plain were hundreds of such groups. Each had a complaint against evil and suffering, God permitted in His world. "How lucky God was to live in heaven with sweetness and light, where there was no weeping or fear no hunger or hatred. What does he know of all that men had been forced to endure in this world? For God leads a pretty life," they said.

So each of these groups sent forth their leader, chosen to speak, because God, they said, had suffered the Jew, a Negro, a person from Hiroshima, a horrible deformed arthritic, a thalidomide child to suffer and die.

In the center of the plain they consulted with each other. At last they were ready to present their case. It was rather clever.

Before God could be qualified to be their judge, he must endure what they had endured. The decision was that God should be sentenced to live on earth---as a man!

"Let him be born a Jew. Let the legitimacy of his birth be doubted.

Give him a work so difficult that even his family will think him out of his mind. Let him be betrayed by his closest friends. Let him face false charges, be tried by a jury and convicted by a cowardly judge. Let him be tortured."

"At the last, let him see what it means to be terribly alone. Then let him die so that no one can doubt he died. Let there be a great host of witnesses to verify it."

As each leader announced his portion of the sentences, loud murmurs of approval went up from the throng of people assembled.

When the last had finished pronouncing sentence, there was a long silence. No one uttered another word. No one moved.

For suddenly all knew that GOD HAD ALREADY SERVED HIS SENTENCE.[113]

The point for me is that in responding to human arrogance, God might seem silent, but such silence does not diminish the reality of God's ability to respond. God judges our earthly histories while He suffers with us in moments when we are put to silence. It was not only in Herod's or Pilate's or in Annas' and Caiphas'

[113] "The Long Silence," Http://www.wsite, com/Cool20180s3.html.

judgment halls and on the cross, but every day in the accusations that Satan heaps against us, God can be silent. He can afford to be for He has suffered for the millennia of earth's history and now has the last word about suffering.

In times when we are accused we can contemplate God's history in the world. We can think of His departure from the courtroom, sometimes it seems God has no word for Himself, and this is what makes the judgment of profound interest. What William Shea says in his brief reflection on Ezekiel 9-11 can be helpful to us. Namely, that when Yahweh comes to His temple for a work of judgment, and when the work of judgment is completed, He departs from His temple and city in silence. Shea's interpretation of the noted passage from Ezekiel is stated thus:

> When Yahweh left His temple He did not depart in the direction from which He came, for He came from the north (Ez 1:4), the direction from which the earthly agents of His judgment - - the Babylonian army - - came. He departed to the east (Ez 10:19; 11:23), in the direction of His exiled people, who should yet return to His land and city, according to the prophecies that follow in Ezekiel.[114]

What is to be said of this departure? Has God abandoned His people? This was the question for the prophets and seems to be the question of the saints to the end of time. But the assurance in scripture is that as the departure of Yahweh from the temple means the destruction of the wicked, so it also means the salvation of the righteous. When Christ left the Jerusalem temple He went to the Mount of Olives, from which He delivered His last great earthly discourse before His crucifixion and took His disciples with Him. After His resurrection He returned to the Mount of Olives, from which He ascended to the heavenly sanctuary or

---

[114] William Shea (1981), "The Investigative Judgment of Judah, Ezekiel 1-10," Studies in The Sanctuary and the Atonement, Biblical, Historical and Theological, eds, A. Wallenkampf and W. R. Lesher (Washington, D.C: Review and Herald), 283-291.

courtroom (Lk 24:50-52; Acts 1:1-12). His departure from the earth is pictured in the Acts and Epistles as the precursor to His inauguration as Lord and Judge (cf. Acts 2:36; Rom 2:16; 2 Tim 4:1). John beautifully pictures the scene of the inauguration in Revelation 4,5. And it is a scene of sounds that breaks all silence.

We can work out the departure from the earth and entry into the heavenly sanctuary courtroom and the dynamics of sounds and silence in more traditional systematic terms. What follows upon the inauguration in the heavenly sanctuary is the scene of judgment (Rev 4:1-8:1). As the author of Hebrews says, "After [Christ] had provided purification for sins, He sat down at the right hand of the Majesty in the heaven" (1:3). "We have such a high priest, who sat down at the right hand of the throne of the Majesty in the heaven, and who serves in the sanctuary, the true tabernacle set up by the Lord, not by man" (8:1).

God is being judged in the judgment

The biblical idea that has led us to the above conclusion is the understanding that the silence in heaven is a reality of judgment, because God judges from a heavenly courtroom in which sound and silence are most profoundly known. The biblical understanding is that God is involved in the judgment, not only as Sovereign and Judge but also as one being judged. In the cosmic history, the story is that God is both Arbiter (Deut 1:17; 2 Tim 1:5) and Arbitee. He is both Judge and Judged. To say this is to note what Karl Barth states so extensively in his Church Dogmatics, that God as Judge is "The Judge judged in our place." He is the one whose righteousness has been called into question. He is the one whose rule has been challenged. His is the one whose character has been maligned. He is the one who through His Son suffered on the cross. For this reason Barth argues that the justification of Jesus Christ is our justification and therefore God's own justification.[115] In the entire act of judgment God at times remains silent, but as Judge and Judged.

Christ is being judged in the judgment

We do not need to make an extensive commentary on the work of Christ in the judgment, except to repeat what has been already noted. Christ is pictured in Scripture as sitting on a glorious throne (Dan 7), as the one worthy to break the seal and open the book of eternal judgment (Rev 5). He is given authority by the Father to participate as Judge and Advocate, Magistrate and Mediator, Sovereign and Guarantor of eternal life. He confronts the accuser of the saints and declares their innocence before the Father. Of this Barth says, "His eternal Word becomes flesh. . . . In order that He may not only conduct His own case against all men, but take up and conduct the case against all men, which they themselves cannot conduct, in that process between Him and them."[116] The point in this is that after Christ has spoken on our behalf, He needs not speak again, except He has a last word to say as Executioner. But we will to return to this last word. Here, we note that His first interest in the courtroom is to settle the question of the righteousness, and through the work of the Holy Spirit and His mission in the Church their cases are being settled.

The righteous are being judged in the judgment

A point of profound assurance to all the saints is that they are not judging themselves, nor is Satan judging them. They are being judged by God, in Jesus Christ (Rom 8). This is the

---

[115] Karl Barth (1956), Church Dogmatics IV:I The Doctrine of Reconciliation (Edinburgh: T & T Clark). In the section on "The Obedience of the Son of God" Barth argues very effectively concerning God as the one who is Judge and the one who is being judged.

[116] Karl Barth (1956), Church Dogmatics IV:I The Doctrine of Reconciliation (Edinburgh: T & T Clark), 551.

perspective from which we can say that God is for us (*pro nobis* to use the Latin phrase which was very loved by Barth).[117] Satan brings an accusation against us, and in the reality of our past behavior we know that Satan is right. But in the reality of the work of Christ on the cross and as Mediator at the throne of justice, we know of a beautiful end to the story of our lives. We do not therefore have to say a word in the courtroom. After we have sent on our confessions through Christ the Judge and Advocate, we can approach the bar with silent confidence. "The Father sent the Son to be the Savior of the world. Therefore our salvation, the salvation of men in the world, takes place in him, in His being and activity as one with us."[118] When God rises up for judgment, He saves all the oppressed of the world (Psa 76:9). The big story is this Jesus became one of us to pronounce us free in the judgment, and therefore He makes our salvation secure.

The wicked are being judged in the judgment

Brief reference must also be made to the case of the wicked who are marked (Hab 1:12) and liable (Matt 5:22) for judgment. Their end reflects the ultimate power over the arrogance of evil. When the Judge shall do His work in His sanctuary, He will mark the wicked for destruction. Satan cannot defend them, and Christ will not speak for them. They will have their after word; but it is only to confess to the justice of God (Rev 16:7; Phil 2:11; Ez 9:15).

After the righteous are judged in the sanctuary of God, God will judge the wicked in the outer court. The separation of the righteous and the wicked, which has taken place in the sanctuary, is complete and final. It means that God does not accept the spurning of His grace. Those who speak against Him are as silent as the idols they have served. Their silence is profound, for the

---

[117] Cf. Ibid., 214.

[118] Ibid., 216.

sentence passed by God is decisive. God is silent as God launches an attack upon their arrogance, their idols and their violence.

Who speaks for God in the judgment?

What I have been pursuing in the underlay of this discussion is "Who speaks for God when God seems to be silent?" When the wicked curse at Him and swear at God, who responds? When God's integrity and God's justice are challenged, who offers a rejoinder? When God's truths are made a mockery, who controverts? When He hangs upon a cross and His enemies pass by and challenge His power by proclaiming "the death of God" who answers for God?

One of the temptations I suffer, and one that is quite popular among Christians, is the temptation to enter into endless debates about God. Often Christians think that they come up with profound rational answers about God; sometimes they think that they can prove the divine existence and the righteousness of God. They think that they are called upon to answer mysterious questions that are not even revealed to them. They even go into court to defend God. It is hard for many to think that God does not need our defense. For in the divine judgment that has taken place in Jesus Christ, God has spoken his last word and it has a binding force.[119] My contention here is that God is not tongue-tied. The silence of the cross did not mean the death of God. Such a silent pause only amplified the sounds of the heavenly activity that was to cause the breaking of the veil of the temple. The God who seemingly had been helpless did a great act in the resurrection, and he will do a great in the last judgment.

At such a time when no more prayers of confessions are to be heard and no more repentance is possible for the wicked, then God is about to do a final act. In effect, God will speak for Himself again. This is the quintessence of what is spoken of in Revelation 8:1 where it says there was silence in heaven for "half

---

[119] Ibid., 570

an hour." God will leave the throne-room, as He left the cross and there was silence.

Fig 3-3

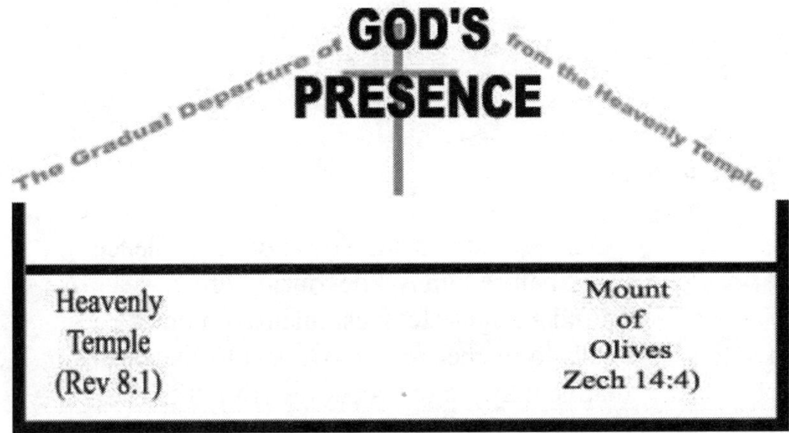

God has spoken for Himself, but will speak again on behalf of the voiceless of the earth who are hoping day and night to hear His voice again. While people face conditions of brutality in this life in which God seems to be silent, there is a call for another word. This is the theme of our discussions to follow.

Our God comes and does not keep silence,
before him is a devouring fire,
And a mighty tempest all around him.
He calls to the heavens above and to the earth,
that he may judge his people (Psa 50:3,4).

V

SILENCE IN HEAVEN AND THE CRY FOR JUSTICE

When he opened the seventh seal, there was silence in heaven for about half an hour. And I saw seven angels who stand before God, and seven trumpets were given to them. Another angel with a golden censer came and stood at the altar; he was given a great quantity of incense to offer with the prayers of the saints on the golden altar that was before the throne. And the smoke of the incense, with the prayers of the saints, rose before God from the hand of the angel. Then the angel took the censer and filled it with fire from the altar and threw it into the earth; and there were peals of thunder, rumblings, flashes of lightning, and an earthquake (Rev 8:1-5).

If God would only answer

It is a great interest for me to do a further reflection on silence with the affirmation that God always answers the prayers of the saints. Let us build into the above text a contradiction of the general view, however, for sometimes the prayers of the saints are not answered, at least not as we wish to have them. In doing a survey of books on the theme of prayer, I come upon themes such as "Incredible Answers to Prayer," "Prevailing Prayers," "Strategies for Prayer Warfare," and other themes of this nature; all bearing the message that our prayers are immediately answered. The common formula for answers we have known is that God says to us "Yes," "No," or "Wait". Dr. Renita Weems, of the School of

Theology at Vanderbilt, adds that sometimes God says "Never."[120] She senses that many saints struggle with the greatest secret questions such as "What happens when it seems like there is silence in heaven?" "What happens when it seems that God is not about to answer?" "What happens when we are being told to be patient and persistent even when no answers are given for a long time?" She senses that sometimes we are tempted to be atheistic, saying that God does not exist. Or that we are persuaded to be sometimes agnostic, saying that we are not sure that God exists. Or even sometimes we feel like being idolatrous, creating our own gods to give us the answers we seek.

The problem that I am confronting in this discussion is not just to ask if God hears the prayers of the saints, but to know why sometimes it seems that God does not answer the prayers of the saints. Why the eternal wait, especially when there is injustice and oppression upon the saints? Why the sometimes helplessness when God is being laughed at, scoffed at, and derided. Why the lack of response when it seems that the world is left in the hands of the wicked? The question generated is, "What about the immediate answer to the prayers of the saints?" The discussion is not asking how effective are prayers in general or the prayers of the saints in particular, but what happens to the saints when there seem to be no immediate answers from heaven? What happens when their souls are being poured out under the altar of death? That was John's question in Revelation 6:9-11 and again in Revelation 8:1-5 with the answer punctuated by silence.

In one of his letters written to his "Silent Confidant" as seen in the compilation Fear and Trembling and Repetition, Soren Kierkegaard notes that he had been standing in silence in one

---

[120] Renita Weems (1999), Listening to God: A Minister's Journey Through Silence and Doubt (New York: Simon & Schuster) is one of the greatest books that I have read on the Christian who struggles on questions of prayer, grace, faith, love, God and mystery. Her transparency is powerful because it causes any true person of faith to face the truth of herself/himself.

position for a whole month. He says he was not sure whether he was standing on his head or standing on his feet. What he was sure of was that he was standing without moving a foot or making a single movement. He was standing speechless and motionless and waiting for a thunderstorm and repetition. He then said he should have been "happy" and "indescribably blessed" if the thunderstorm would have come. For if it came he was sure it would shatter his whole personality, making him fit to be a husband. It would render him almost unrecognizable to himself, save his honor, redeem his pride, and give him some unfailing consolation. But if it did not come he would have to become crafty, faking death so that he could be buried without facing embarrassment for the loss of face.[121] The saints of God often feel like this. They want the thunderstorm, the judgment against wickedness, I mean. They pray and wait for the thunder and the trumpet blast of God, but there is silence, and they often wonder why, when, whether there is to be an answer. Has God forgotten them?

The larger text around Revelation 8:1 is that which has dragged me into this kind of reflection on silence in heaven and the prayers of the saints. While it notes that there are seven angels standing at the altar before God with seven trumpets given to them, and one angel standing with a golden censer of incense and the prayers of the saints, it does not tell us how long before the prayers of the saints are answered and the censers, which are filled with fire, will be thrown into the earth. The time of waiting when rational thought says, maybe God has not, will not, or does not care to answer is often filled with apprehension. Reason and critical reflection are gifts of God, but have their limits, and struggle for the divine manifestation, especially when they are confronting oppression, thus, the cry for justice.

---

[121] Soren Kierkegaard (1983), Fear and Trembling, Repetition, Howard Hong and Edna Hong editors and translators, (New Jersey: Princeton University Press), 214-215.

The cry for justice

When the saints confront the tragedy of injustice in the land, when they see the prejudice, oppression, persecution and affliction perpetuated against them and against humanity in general, they are pressed to ask, "Sovereign Lord, holy and true, *how long* will it be before you avenge our blood on the inhabitants of the earth?" (Rev 6:10), (Emphasis mine). Here is how the theme runs through the Scripture, "How Long, O Lord? Will you forget me [us] forever? How long will you hide your face from me (us)?" (Psa. 13:1) (My pluralization). "How long, O Lord, will you look on? Rescue me from their ravages, my life from the lions!" (Psa. 35:17). "How long, O Lord? Will you be angry forever? Will your jealous wrath burn like fire?" (Psa. 79:5). "How long, O Lord? Will you hide yourself forever? How long will your wrath burn like fire?" (Psa. 89:46). "Turn, O Lord! How long? Have compassion on your servants!" (Psa. 90:13). "O Lord! How long shall the wicked exult?" (Psa. 94:3) "How long, O Lord . . . . until cities lie waste without inhabitants, and houses without people and the land is utterly desolate?" (Isa. 6:11). "Our Lord, how long shall I cry for help, and you will not listen? Or cry to you 'Violence!' and you will not save?" (Hab. 1:2). "How long will it take for the vision to be fulfilled – the vision concerning the daily sacrifice, the rebellion that causes desolation, and the surrender of the sanctuary and the host that will be trampled underfoot?" (Dan 8:13 NIV). "Then the angel of the Lord said, 'O Lord of hosts, how long will you withhold mercy from Jerusalem and the cities of Judah, with which you have been angry these seventy years?'" (Zec 1:12). The saints are often challenged with their silent fears, and disheartened with their silent tears. "Sometimes" they find "the shadows are deep and rough seems the path to the goal." While they pray they incur silence, or so it seems. They ask for an answer and receive none, or so it seems. As Samuel T. Lloyd III says, "The otherness and immensity of silence present us with a reality beyond our control or understanding . . . ." "It is not easy even for an earnest seeker after God to know what to make of the silence of prayer." The only question such a person keeps asking is "Why is . . . God so elusive, so silent?"[122]

The cry for justice and the test of faith

The underlay to the question we are discussing is that God's seeming silence to evil brings the test of faith to the saints. I have often tried to imagine what John must have felt when he was brought to Rome from Asia Minor by Emperor Domitian, then beaten and imprisoned, then, according to tradition, taken and thrown into a caldron of boiling oil and, when through the grace of God he was spared that fate of death, he was banished to Patmos for hard labor. Some tradition even has it that while in Ephesus John was stoned by the followers of Artemis because he denounced idol and demon worship. When I read John's words about the saints crying under the altar, I think of John himself and the millions of other saints and innocents who have suffered at the hands of wicked people. When demonic violence rages in every corner of the earth and nothing seems to be able to stop it, my existential being gets caught up with the saints and the Psalmist to pray, "Remember O Lord that your enemies laugh at you, that they are godless and despise you . . . There is violence in every dark corner of the land . . . (Psa 78:18, 20). Many saints have told me that sometimes, hearing the words, "wait a little longer, until the number of your fellow servants which are to be killed is completed." (Rev 6:10) really challenges their mind? Such a response often seems like a double-edged sword, for in the midst of waiting for the manifestation of God, patience runs out (Rev 14:12). The point is that as the saints wait to see the final manifestation of God, their last great temptation will be raised in the question, "Can God be trusted to bring the great controversy to a conclusion? Just when/how will God do it?" The cry "How long,

---

122 Lloyd, Samuel T. III, "The Silence of Prayer," Sewanee Theological Review 35:2 (1992) 158-172.

O Lord? Will you forget us forever? How long will you hide your face from us? How long must we wrestle with our thoughts and every day have sorrow in our hearts? How long will our enemies triumph over us? Look at us and answer, O Lord our God" (cf. Psa 13:1-3 NIV),[123] is not a flippant cry. It is the most persistent sentence in the prayers of the saints. As the slaves of North America tried to anticipate liberation they used to say:

> My brother, how long
> Fore we done suffering here?
> It won't be long,
> Fore the Lord call us home[124]

In the midst of the suspense the saints hold on to the belief that God is faithful. That God is a God of justice. That God is the providential one. That God is the merciful one. But such assurances sometimes seem to run into a crisis. Thus the point needs to be made that it is Satan who is seeking to destroy the faith of the saints. He troubles the saints about the difficulty of forgiveness. He states that, "There are limitations concerning God's actions in the world. He suggests that God is powerful, but not all powerful, God is good, but not all good. God is love, but not all love." "Satan has come to them [the saints] disguised as an angel of light, and under his direction the majority of Christians bow at idolatrous shrines and worship an unknown God. . . ."[125] Satan's work has been to get the saints to distrust God in the time between sound and silence.

---

[123] I have changed the pronouns to plural in the text to reflect the fellow feeling of all the saints who I think at some point in their souls' trials identify with the Psalmist.

[124] Thomas Higgerson (1979), Been in a Storm So Long: The Aftermath of Slavery (New York: Vintage Books), 104.

[125] Ellen White (1999), Christ Triumphant (Hagerstown, MD: Review and Herald), 279 (Quoted from Manuscript 63, 1897).

Why sometimes the saints do not hear God

Sometimes it is not silence that the saints are hearing but their own voices. Satan often presses upon the saints' anxieties, and leads them in resentment and self-pity, and allows them to speak continually so that they cannot hear God speaking back to them. Their dialogue with God becomes a monologue when they alone speak and God is expected to listen all the time. They forget that they stand before a God who can speak. They think that his only function is to listen. Soren Kierkegaard says that the important thing in prayer, the important thing to concentrate upon is not so much that God hears what we pray for, but that we pray until we hear what God's will is.[126]

Another problem we confront in the delayed answers in our prayers is that Satan always tries to put together agents, or circumstances, which stand in opposition to God, so that answers are delayed. The story of Daniel is a great illustration of this. In telling the story of the great controversy Daniel records the exploits of "the little horn" (Daniel 7:25f). He states that it is a quintessential demonic power, which seeks to corrupt the truth of God, desecrate the center of divine worship, and "raise itself" (himself) to challenge the very throne of God. Daniel is distressed concerning the display of the evil power because such display is worse than being cast into the Lion's den. Daniel finds assurance in the fact that God releases two holy ones from heaven who pick up the heart-cry of Daniel. One holy one says to the other, "[How long, O Lord] for how long is the vision concerning the continual burnt offering, the transgression that makes desolate, and the giving of the sanctuary and the host to be trampled under foot?" (Dan 8:13). Then Daniel receives the answer, "For two thousand and three hundred evenings and mornings; then shall the sanctuary be restored to its rightful place" (Dan 8:14). The rest of the story that leads into Daniel 9 and 10 tells how Daniel's distress grew

---

[126] Ibid., 259.

worse because of what he had seen in the earlier part of the vision and by what he had just heard. Even though the angel Gabriel was dispatched to assure Daniel that God listens to the prayers of the saints, and that in the final judgment, the saints will be righted, yet Daniel's anguish remains. He is told that there is a continuance of satanic activity against the people of God. While God is at work Satan also works. In chapter 9:1-2 Daniel reveals that by reading the book of Jeremiah (cf. Jer 25:11f) he has come to understand that the length of time for the oppressive actions of the enemy against the people of God is seventy years (cf. Jer 29:7, 10). He thus prays - - confesses and supplicates - - on behalf of himself and his people, hoping that the time will be shortened. Throughout the prayer Daniel notes that God is a God of mercy as He is a God of wrath (cf. Dan 9:3-19). He recognizes that it is by grace that all humanity is spared from wrath. But when Daniel prays, and the Angel Gabriel is dispatched and cannot come, Daniel is distressed.

The delay expresses the reality that we have been seeking to discuss. Sometimes the prayers of the saints are answered in expeditious ways, while at other times there are delays. As one young saint said to me, some time ago, "I cannot see any sense in this." I failed my exam, I had to do the work all over again, and now I can't see why". In the same way when the angel was delayed Daniel became profoundly distressed and lost his speech. The specific answer to the prayer that was supposed to remove some of Daniel's anxiety was:

> Seventy weeks are determined for your people and for your holy city, to finish the transgression, to put an end to sin, and to atone for iniquity, to bring in everlasting righteousness, to seal both vision and prophet, and to anoint the most holy place. Know therefore and understand: from the time that the word went out to restore and rebuild Jerusalem until the time of an anointed prince, there shall be seven weeks; and for sixty-two weeks it shall be built again with streets and moat, but in a troubled time. After

> the sixty-two weeks an anointed one shall be cut off and shall have nothing, and the troops of the prince that is to come shall destroy the city and the sanctuary. Its end shall come with a flood and to the end there shall be war. Desolations are decreed. He shall make a strong covenant with many for one week, and for half of the week he shall make sacrifice and offering cease; and in their place shall be the abomination that desolates, until the decreed end is poured upon the desolate (Dan 9:24-27).

This prophecy of seventy weeks of years has been variously interpreted. One view accepted by a large group of respected scholars is that it represents a prophetic time- line, cut off from the two thousand three hundred days of years of Daniel 8:14, which makes reference to God's great work of judgment that is to take place from the heavenly temple in the end time.[127] The seventy weeks is the time allotted in the Jewish economy of salvation, at the end of which time the Messiah would come to renew the covenant. Thus when Christ came and began His preaching with the words "The time is fulfilled, and the kingdom of God is at hand, repent and believe the gospel," (Mk 1:15) He was speaking of this prophecy of Daniel. He indicated that the present economy of salvation had become bankrupt and that He had come to bring an end to sin, make reconciliation for iniquity, and bring in everlasting righteousness. According to the prophetic interpretation, 490 years began in 457 BCE and ended in 34 ACE. The anointing of the Messiah took place in 27 ACE, that is, when Christ was baptized and the voice spoke from heaven, "This is my beloved with whom I am well pleased." The ministry of Christ was to be for the last of the seventy weeks. "In the midst of the

---

[127] Cf. Henry L. Rudy (1981), The Message of Revelation: An Exposition of the Book of Revelation, Volume 2, (College Place, Washington, Color Press); Mervyn Maxwell (1981-1985), God Cares: The Message of Revelation for You and Your Family in 2 Vols. (Boise, ID: Pacific Press).

week," that is, in 31 ACE, the Messiah "was cut off," or crucified. Three and a half years later, that is, 34 ACE, the gospel was being proclaimed to the Gentiles (Acts 8:4). In effect, the time of Christ's coming, His anointing, His death and resurrection and the giving of the gospel to the nations were all pointed out. All the Gospel writers insist on this. They argue that the advent of Christ, His ministry and death has signified the beginning of the great eschatological speech of God. Thus when Jesus announced His intention to start His journey to Jerusalem and to face His executioners, Satan did everything to prevent Him (Matt 16:21-23).

In my mind there is a connection between what occurred in Daniel 10, in which case the prince of Persia detained for twenty-one days the ministering angel who was sent to respond to Daniel's prayer, and the anxieties of the saints to hear God speak in the last days. Demonic forces will establish agencies and build up circumstances so that the messages of comfort and hope intended for God's people will not reach them for weeks, months, and maybe years. But the people of God are to be thankful that no matter how hard the demons try to stop the messages of comfort and encouragement that Michael, the archangel who wrestles against the forces of evil so that Daniel could receive the answer to his prayers, will come in the end time to destroy all evil. In using R. H. Charles' comment to make a point that I consider most profound, William Barclay states that the needs of the saints are more to God than all the psalmody of heaven, so God pauses for half an hour (Rev 8:1) to listen to their prayers.[128]

For Markus Barth by sending Jesus (i.e. the Michael of Daniel) God made humanity's business his business. He gave away the best and dearest He has, His Son, for the redemption of humanity. At the cross, God openly stood against sin, and not only against sin, but God stood against Himself, the Father against the Son. When the Father was addressed in Jesus' prayer, He

---

[128] William Barclay (1976), The Revelation of John vol. 2, (Philadelphia: The Westminster Press), 126.

responded with justice and mercy.[129] So in the crisis of silence at the end the saints can shake themselves with the assurance that even though God's answer is slow, and mysterious, and might have us wait into eternity, yet it is sure. As the prophets insisted, "Evil doers shall be cast down" (cf. Psa 35:17; 90:13; 91; 94:3). God "kills and brings life, forces into the pit and brings out." He "kills and makes alive." He "wounds and heals." He "establishes kings" and "puts them down." God destroy all people who are inimical to Him. He executes them as He seeks to destroy all evil.[130] So it is not that God does not have an answer, but in our frame the answers are long delayed. In one of the world's most loved religious poems as written by Ophelia Guyon Browning, our idea is supported thus:

Unanswered, Yet the prayer lips have pleaded
In agony of heart these many years?
Does faith begin to fail, is hope declining.
And think you all in vain those falling tears?
Say not the Father has not heard your prayer;
You may have your desire, sometime, somewhere.

Unanswered yet? Tho' when you first presented
This one petition at the Father's throne,
It seemed you could not wait the time of asking,
So anxious was your heart to have it done;
If years have passed since them, do not despair,
For God will answer you sometime, somewhere.

Unanswered yet? But you are not unheeded;
The promises of God forever stand;
To him our day and years are equal;
Have faith in God! It is your Lord's command.
Hold on to Jacob's angel, and your prayer

---

[129] Markus Barth (1971), Justification (Grand Rapids, MI: Wm. B. Eerdmans), 39.
[130] Ibid., 17.

Shall bring a blessing down sometime, somewhere.

Unanswered yet? Nay, do not say unanswered,
Perhaps your part is not yet wholly done,
The work began when first your prayer was uttered,
And God will finish what he has begun.
Keep incense at the shrine of prayer,
And glory shall descend sometime somewhere.

Unanswered yet? Faith cannot be unanswered;
Her feet are firmly planted on the Rock;
Amid the wildest storms she stands undaunted,
Nor quails before the loudest thunder shock.
She knows Omnipotence has heard her prayer,
And cries, "It shall be done sometime, somewhere."

Eternity will give us answers of which we have never dreamed

In effect, when facing the divine silence the saints of God, with their prophetic faith, will find that their faith is bound up with the destiny of history. They will find that God's time is not their time. They will find that the Jesus who is celebrated in Scripture as our Great High Priest (see Rev 4, 5; Heb 5-10) has not forsaken them. Even when probation closes they will still be able to pray, for prayers are not only confessions but also the heart's cry for the manifestation of God. They are prayers of thanksgiving (*eucharisteo*) and prayers of adoration (*proskuneo*) and the call for judgment against the present evils of the world. They are prayers for the coming of the Kingdom. John Phillips well says of the saints' prayers:

> What a potent force is prayer! The saints go into their bedrooms, close the doors, kneel down, and pray. They spread out before God their petitions, and God hears. The prayers are placed in the scales of judgment. In some

mysterious way not explained to us, "prayer changes things." This is true in every age. In a coming day, as the saints pray, "the angel of the Lord" (surely the Lord Himself) will come forward and add to the groans and cries the perfume and the fragrance of His finished work. For prayer never reaches God in the clumsy, inept, feeble way it leaves our lips. The Holy Spirit's energizing of our prayers and the risen Lord's endorsement of our prayers make them a force to be reckoned with in the universe. So then, [while] there is silence in heaven for half an hour . . . God graciously takes into consideration the prayers of his own.[131]

Answers for the saints, silence for the wicked

What we have been trying to show throughout our discussion is that in spite of the challenges of the heavenly silence for the saints, they can hold to the assurance that God is ever sympathetic to their situation and always has an answer for them. They know of times when Satan has reduced their voices to a whisper. Times when they try to pray and nothing comes forth from their lips but muffled sounds. Times when Satan brings strange burdens upon them. Sometimes he takes the speech away and makes it seem that God has abandoned us. But in the midst of his effort to confound, we can hear a calm voice that says, "Hold on a little longer my friends. Hold on a little longer and don't give in. Jesus has promised your shelter to be. Just hold on a little longer my friends."[132]

---

[131] John Phillips (1974, 1987), Exploring Revelation, (Chicago: Moody Press), 118.

[132] I heard these words many years ago sung by the Chuck Fulmore family, I have not been in contact with them much, but I always remember their story that the words were written upon the death of their son, who killed in a car crash.

We shall return in a later discussion with a further commentary on the encouragement of the saints, but we turn here to introduce our connecting discussion by making the point that when the wicked experience the heavenly silence and seek to hear God speak, they will not have any answer. They may try to get a word from a prophet of God, but find "famine" for a word from God (cf. Ez 7:26). They will try to find peace, but there will be no peace to the wicked says the Lord (cf. Ez 7:25). They will try to look for someone to save them, but there will be no one (cf. 1 Sam 22:42). They will cry out to the rocks, but the rocks cannot answer them (cf. 1 Sam 8:18). The point is that they have not listened to God, and now God will not listen to them. They have not used the time allotted them for repentance, and now their cry is only that of consternation. They know no confidence of communication. They only know the silence of their idols. They will cry to their idols, which cannot hear them. As the prophet Habakkuk says, "What use is an idol once its maker has shaped it – cast image, a teacher of lies, for its maker trusts in what has been made, though the product is only an idol that cannot speak! Alas for you say to the wood 'wake up,' to silent stone 'Rouse yourself!' Can it teach? See, it is gold and silver and there is no breath in it at all. But the Lord is in his holy temple, let all the earth keep silence before him!" (Hab 2:18-20).

There is judgment when God responds to the prayers of the saints

In effect, the saints who have put their trust in God will always have answers from the divine. Even though God permits the wicked to carry forward their violence against the saints, and even against His throne, God never leaves unanswered the prayers of the saints. In the story of the Exodus which we shall reference often in this part of our reflection it is noted that:

> After a long time the king of Egypt died. The Israelites groaned under their slavery and cried out. Out of the slavery their cry for help rose up to God. God heard their groaning, and God remembered his covenant with Abraham, Isaac, and Jacob. God looked upon the Israelites, and God noticed them (Ex 2:23-25).

The intervention of God is very carefully emphasized in the text. As Donald E. Gowan says, "In response to the Israelites' outcry (*za`aq, shawa`*), God is said to have *heard* their groaning, *remembered* his covenant, *seen* the Israelites, and *known* without an object in the Hebrew text; RSV supplies "their condition"; NRSV uses "took notice of them."[133] The response that follows the silent moment of Revelation 8:1 is quite similar to the response in the story of the Exodus. John indicates as the rising smoke of the incense with the prayers of the saints (Rev 8:3), and the angel with the censer filled with fire from God's altar to be cast into the earth (Rev 8:4,5). In commenting upon the latter Matthew Henry says that the censer in the hand of the angel contains fire and incense which sanctifies the prayers of all the saints. He also argues that when the voice of God comes from the golden altar, it is the voice that commands for the release of the four angels bound at the river Euphrates. Henry feels that the altar is probably the same altar under which the martyrs of Revelation 6:9 are. He also believes the imagery of the incense picks up from Exodus 30:7, where we find that incense was burned day and night upon a golden altar. In Heb 9:3 it is stated that the earthly altar of incense was in the most holy place next to the Ark of the Covenant. He also points to the fact that the references to the golden censer and golden altar reflect on the purity and value of the prayers of the saints. The scroll in the hand of the Lamb (Rev 5:8) is also connected to the golden bowls full of incense with the prayers of

---

[133] Donald E. Gowan (1994), Theology in Exodus: Biblical Theology in Form of a Commentary, Louisville, Ken.: Westminster John Knox Press, 5.

the saints. The prayers of the saints are therefore a key to the fulfillment of God's plan.[134]

The Scripture point to the fact that God is waiting for the saints to pray as Jesus prayed, "Your kingdom come, your will be done on earth and it is in heaven" (Matt 6:10). The phrase in Revelation 8, which states that the prayers of the saints "went up before God," indicates that God hears the prayers of all His people.[135] The comparison is clear with God's hearing of the cry of the Israelites when they were in slavery in Egypt (Exo 2:23, 3:9). As one reads the introductory piece to the Exodus one might argue that God had been absent from the picture for a while. In fact, the people of God seemed to have been in struggle without the needed help from God. The midwives seemed to have been leading a resistance with a little help from God, but in the main, it seemed that God was outside of the story. And then as the people continued to "groan" God heard and answered.[136] In effect, whenever the church on earth confronts oppression, and the saints cry, heaven listens, and the saints can wait in silent expectation for God has answers.[137]

When the prayers of the saints are accepted in heaven, they produce great changes upon earth. The strange commotions of thunderings, lightnings, and great earthquakes that we hear in the earth, are often God's answers to the prayers of the saints. These are only a few of the answers God gives to the prayers of the saints. His tokens of anger against the wicked are many and can be intense, and the saints can trust to their demonstration.[138].

---

[134] Matthew Henry (1961 edition), Concise Commentary on the Whole Bible: Revelation (Grand Rapids, MI.: Zondervan).

[135] Ibid.

[136] Donald E. Gowan (1994), Theology in Exodus: Biblical Theology in Form of a Commentary, Louisville, Ken.: Westminster John Knox Press, p. 5.

[137] Matthew Henry (1961 edition), Concise Commentary on the Whole Bible: Revelation (Grand Rapids, MI.: Zondervan).

[138] Ibid.

In essence, what is stated in the covenant promises will be fulfilled. To Abraham God said, "I will bless those who bless you, and the ones who curse you I will curse" (Gen 12:3). As the blessings have been seen in the history of God's people, so also the curses have been seen upon those who have sought to curse the people of God. Some of the outstanding stories in Scripture that record the curses are of interest. When, for example, the Egyptians tried to curse Israel God sent ten plagues upon the Egyptians (cf. Exo 7:14-13:32). The story of Balaam who joined with Balak to curse God's people is also notable. Balaam was so cursed that in his final oracle he issued his own condemnation (cf. Num 24:17), and then when Israel went to war with Midian, it was noted that Balaam was also killed (Num 30:7,8). In the book of Esther is recorded the curse upon Haman. Haman planned to have Mordicai hanged and the Jews killed, but it is Haman who was disgraced and hanged (Esther 5-7). Isaiah was records the story of king Sennacherib who threatened Jerusalem and mocked the God of heaven. In response to the prayers of Israel, God struck the Assyrian army so that one hundred eighty five thousand of them died. Later Sennacherib was also struck by two of his bodyguards who escaped into the land of Ararat (cf. Isa 36-37). The point here is that in as much as God blesses the saints so He curses those who curse the saints. When I was young I used to hear people says "I am going to pray a bad prayer for you." Their curse was a bad wish or a bad prayer. They thought that they were in control of the forces of life and could control them against a person. They never thought that God could turn a curse against all vengeful wishers or prayers. In the end of history, as is told in Revelation, when the enemies of God surround the camp of the saints to bring their destruction, fire will come down from God out of heaven to consume the enemies (Rev 20:9).

Whenever the saints are tempted to think that God is not attending their sufferings, and that such sufferings have no good purpose, they can look to God's covenant promise that God will bless them as He curses their enemies. The armies of Pharaoh may come (Ex 14), the thunders may roll, the lightning may flash, the earth may quake, and the veil of the heavenly temple may be rent in two, but it is certain that God will not leave a case of His interest alone without a great resolution. God always responds to the prayers of the saints, and the universe always experiences the direct intervention of God.[139] Sometime what God is doing cannot be explained, but those who read God's purpose in faith will be satisfied that God is acting. An old Latin hymn written in 1695 and put to music by Giovanni P. da Palestrina (1525-1594) says it well:

> The powers of death have done their worst,
> And Jesus hath his foes dispersed.
> Let shouts of praise and joy outburst.
> Alleluia!
>
> On that third morn he rose again
> In glorious majesty to reign;
> O let us swell the joyful strain.
> Alleluia!
>
> He closed the yawning gates of hell,
> The bars from heaven's highest portals fell;
> Let songs of joy his triumph tell.
> Alleluia!

What has been said is this. The answers to the prayers of the saints, which sometimes seem mystifying in this life, will find their fullest explanation in the life that is to come. As the judgment will put the ultimate question of all satanic pretensive claims to rest, so will be opened for the saints, answers that they could not imagine in this life. The God who spoke, the God who acted, the God who stood with His people against Satan, will always speak, and act and stand for them. God has heard the cry of

---

[139] Ibid., 35-50.

the saints who prayed and waited through the silences of life. He will judge and vindicate His name, and the curse will cease (Rev 22:3). As a consequence the oppressors of the righteous will be brought to silence.

VI

AFTER THE CALM A STORM: THE JUDGMENT OF THE WICKED

After the calm a storm: Announcing the time of God's battle

> It's the calm before the storm, the calm before the storm
> Night's darkest hour is right before dawn
> Calm before the storm, calm before the storm
> Don't hesitate and fight the war . . . [140]

It is the calm before the storm. One who has lived or traveled within the path of a storm, a hurricane, a typhoon, or a tornado can speak of the dramatic contrast between the calm and the violent winds that blow. Sometimes the violence is short and intense and at other times long and ferocious. However the winds may be, there is often great disruption and loss of life. The saying, "After a calm a storm" suitably describes the difference between the "silence in heaven for the space of half an hour," which signals the salvation of the saints, the sounds of trumpets and the other extraordinary sounds that signal the destruction of the wicked. It is the calm before the storm.

---

[1] http://www.kcs.com.au/~boomdocks/lyrics/valm4.htm, I have only noted a verse of Yoko Ono's popular song "Levelheads Lyrics . . . Calm Before the Storm" to make the point here that one should not think that Yahweh's silence means that Yahweh is powerless in the world. The Bible clearly teaches that through His providential power Yahweh is always in charge of the world and that one of these days Yahweh will "roar" from Zion (cf. Amos 1:2; cf. Jer 25:30), and bring His great tempest of fire upon the earth (Jer 11:16).

Before reexamining my text of reference, let me quote the prophetic inquiry presented in the book of Isaiah concerning God's desire to break His silence. This illustrates my point that often after the judgment of His people reflected by His silence, God brings judgment upon the wicked and speaks in thunderous speech to draw their attention. The inquiry reads, "Is it because I have long been silent that you have not feared me?" The prophetic warning follows the inquiry, namely: "I will expose your righteousness and your works, and they will not benefit you. When you cry out for help, let your collection of idols save you! The wind will carry them off; a mere breath will blow them away. But the Man who makes me his refuge will inherit the land and possess my holy mountain." (Isa 57:11 lp.–13 NIV). This can serve to introduce us to the contrast between the silence and the sounds of the judgment as they come to us following Revelation 8:1:

> When the Lamb opened the seventh seal, there was silence in heaven for about half an hour. And I saw seven angels who stand before God, and seven trumpets were given to them. Another angel with a golden censer came and stood at the altar; he was given a great quantity of incense to offer with the prayers of the saints on the golden altar that was before the throne. And the smoke of the incense, with the prayers of the saints, rose before God from the hand of the angel. Then the angel took the censer and filled it with fire from the altar and threw it into the earth; and there were peals of thunder, rumblings, flashes of lightning, and an earthquake (Rev 8:1-5).

Here, John utilizes the great historical symbol of the trumpet, which as we said, introduces the Day of Atonement or other great activities as they took place in ancient cultures. He uses the sounds of the trumpet sounds of judgment as they follow the heavenly silence. For William Barclay such is most appropriate:

> . . . In the visions of the Old and the New Testament the trumpet is always the symbol of the intervention of God in history. All these pictures, and there are many of them, go back to the scene at Mount Sinai, when the law was given to the people. There were on the mountain thunders and lightnings and thick cloud, and a very loud trumpet blast (Exodus 19: 16,19). This trumpet blast became an unchanging part of the apparatus of the Day of the Lord. In that day the great trumpet will be blown and it will summon back the exiles from every land (Isaiah 27:13). On the Day of the Lord the trumpet will be blown in Zion and the alarm sounded in the holy mountain (Joel 2:1). That day will be a day of trumpet and alarm (Zephaniah 1:16). The Lord will blow the trumpet and go out with the whirlwind (Zechariah 9:14).[141]

Barclay notes further that this is the time of God's battle.[142] It is the time of God's judgments. Between the judgment of the saints and the judgment of the wicked there is a time of silence. The silence (or silences) comes (come) between the time of the seals, (and) the sounds of the seven trumpets, the seven thunders, the seven woes, and the seven last plagues. Each pause calls humanity to a moment to repent (cf. Rev 8:2 ff.). But when the time of God's mercy has been offered (Rev 14:6,7) and the word of warning is rejected (Rev 14:8), then it is the end of God's silence for there is to be decisive word (Rev 14:9-11). As the divine word came out of silence at creation, and on the morning of resurrection, so again He will come out of silence for His final word. Through the prophet Isaiah we hear the following inquiry, "Have I not kept silent and closed my eyes, and so you do not fear me?" And the response of judgment is given as, "I will concede your righteousness and your works, but they will not help you.

---

[141] William Barclay (1976), The Revelation of John Vol. 2 (Philadelphia: Westminster Press), 42.

[142] Ibid., 42, 43.

When you cry out, let your collection of idols deliver you. The wind will carry them off, a breath will take them away" (Isa 57:11-13). The time of the divine silence is the divine rebuke and His executive word of judgment.

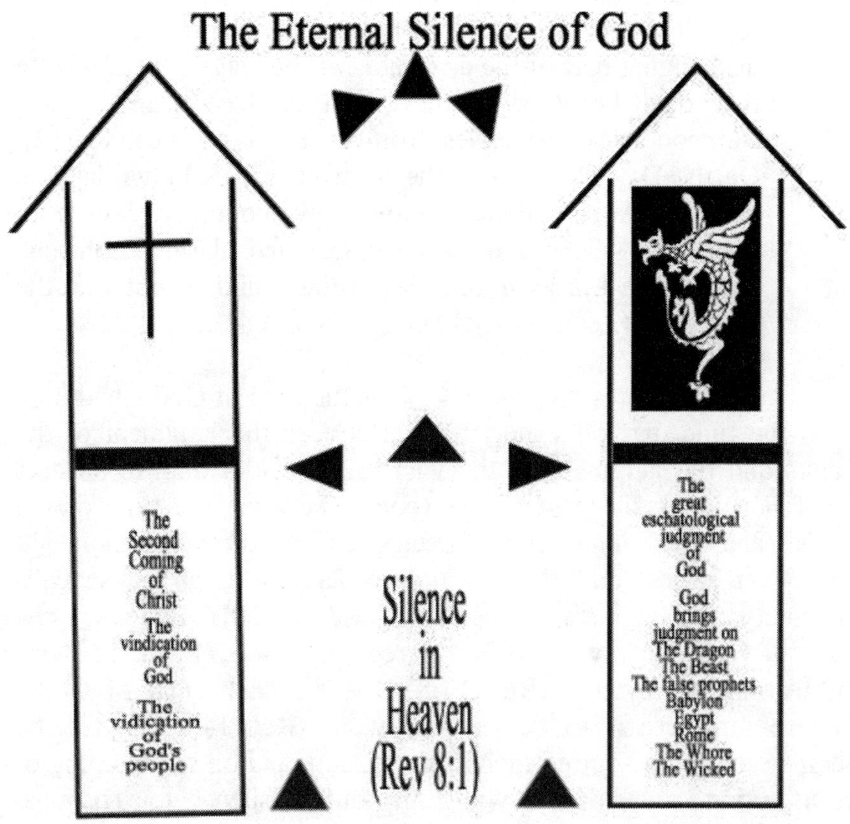

When God breaks His silence there is judgment upon the wicked

The judgment of God is in response to humanity's rejection of the His mercy and the prayers of the saints. God reacts to the blasphemies against his name and God's regard for the persecution of His people. As the biblical authors have stated:

> Our God comes and does not keep silence, before Him is a devouring fire and a mighty tempest all around Him. He calls to the heavens above and to the earth, that He may judge His people: "Gather to me my faithful ones who made a covenant with me by sacrifice!" The heavens declare His righteousness, for God Himself is judge (Psa 50:3-6).

> Then the sign of the Son of Man will appear in heaven, and then all the tribes of the earth will mourn, and they will see "the Son of Man coming on the clouds of heaven" with power and great glory. And he will send out his angels with a loud trumpet call and they will gather his elect from the four winds, from one end of the heaven to the other. (Matt 24:30, 31).

> And I saw the seven angels who stand before God, and seven trumpets were give to them . . . Now the seven angels were given the seven trumpets made ready to blow them. (Rev 8:2, 6).

These and other biblical texts speak to the contrast of the silence of salvation as noted in Revelation 8:1 and the sounds of judgment that are to follow. The silence connects the seven seals with the seven trumpets. When the seven trumpets are to be sounded, the Savior will depart from His sanctuary. The departure ushers in the palpable silence, which we argued, follows the angels' call to repentance. Then in the final act of judgment the voice of God and the angels with the sounds of trumpets is heard in the open heavens. The most solemn of words, "*It is finished,*" spoken in the ears of a startled universe from the cross, will be spoken again (Rev 16:17). These words of finality are God's final words of judgment. They are what Karl Barth liked to call God's Y*es* and *No* against humanity. In this connection Barth says, "The sentence of God passed in His judgment is a decisive sentence."[143] And when God has completed His act there are no half-measures.[144] Oswald Chambers says that God has spoken His last words in the redemption of humanity.[145] God then enters into the silence that will initiate the execution of the wicked. The silence is the transition between the judgment of salvation that has been effected and the judgment of execution that is to be completed. It is the movement from the investigative to the executive judgment.

From the biblically supported schema as it develops in Revelation 8:1 and subsequent passages, the work of the judgment reaches its ultimate stage. John outlines the sounding of the trumpet as portentous of the consummation. Vernard Eller says, John has worked things so as to bring the interlude out at the same point as the seventh seal. Thus, having portrayed the expansiveness and fullness of the Church of the living, the victory of the Church of those who have died, and the life of the Church that is yet to come, John is ready to return to the seal sequence and complete it with the seventh. In effect, John handles it in a very brief compass, bringing us to the end but not actually describing it. John's purpose is apparent, Eller argues that he is not yet ready to proceed into the end and beyond it, because he has in mind at this point to double back and present more material regarding the end-time period – in this case under the series of the seven trumpets. With the seventh seal, then, John is locating the end but not yet exploring it. From here Eller argues that the *half an hour* of silence is the hush which signals that the world is to enter into "God's Evil hour" and the appropriate time of cessation, quietness,

---

[143] Karl Barth (1956), Church Dogmatics IV:I The Doctrine of Reconciliation (Edinburgh, T & T Clark),
568.

[144] Ibid., 569.

[145] Oswald Chambers (1935), My Utmost for His Highest (Uhrichsville, OH: Barbour & Co. Inc), 326.

and rest, the heavenly Sabbath rest.[146] In the remainder of this chapter we will briefly explore the divine response to the manifestation of evil among the wicked, while in a concluding discussion we focus on the silence of the heavenly Sabbath and the new heavenly sounds.

If we analyze the textual chronology which is presented in Revelation 4-7, we will find upon reaching Revelation 8:1ff that the investigative judgment, which proceeds from the heavenly courtroom and focuses on the saints, has already been completed and that now an executive judgment which attends to the wicked will be accomplished outside the courtroom. The executive judgment is God's final response to the satanic evil that has been displayed in the history of the earth (cf. Rev 8:3-4). God will challenge the arrogance of the wicked that deride His name and laugh at His people. Thus an angel takes the prayer censer and fills it with fire from the golden altar and throws it into the earth. Peals of thunder, rumblings, flashes of lightning and a great earthquake will follow, signifying the closing moments of the great eschatological judgment of God. This is the second trajectory of the judgment. It is a judgment of liberation and a judgment of execution. Markus Barth says that for a long time and with almost inconceivable patience God has kept silent in the face of the ravings of the godless; but now He finally rises up in flaming anger. He summons all Jews and Gentiles to assemble before his throne, in order to expose "all ungodliness and unrighteousness of men who suppress the truth by their unrighteousness", and to see to it that they harvest what they have sown. He is now to prove himself to be "judge over the world." The saints moan "How long O Lord, how long?" They have experienced the silence of God and issue a desperate or furious cry for the appearance of God. At last God waits no longer, but manifests Himself to exercise his royal prerogative. Earlier acts of judgment concerned individual men,

---

[146] Eller Vernard (1974), The Most Revealing Book of the Bible (Grand Rapids, MI.: Wm. B. Eerdmans),
104, 105.

Israel, or at most, some of the nations; this time God is judging the whole earth and every human being together. God's judgment is unconditional while the judges of earth can only judge conditionally. While there are many judges who handle the laws of earth and use their power within the jurisdictions entrusted to them, God judge the universe, including the judges, petty and supreme. God has jealously kept the final judgment for himself. Since no one can cope with all of the unrighteousness and injustice of the world and master it, God must enter in.[147]

Seven angels blowing seven trumpets

When the seven angels of Revelation 8:2 are dispatched from the heavenly court to blow the seven trumpets, their blowing signal the final day of God's wrath. On most occasions where the trumpet blast is recorded in Scripture there is a signal of judgment. The following some of the occasions:

i. To announce the coming of God to Mt. Sinai, (Ex 19:16).
ii. To announce the coronation of the king (Solomon), (1 King 1:34).
iii. To announce the winning of a battle, (1 Sam 13:3).
iii. To announce the Israelites entry into Jericho, (Josh 6:3-9).
iv. To announce the second coming of Christ, (1 Thess 4:16, Zep 1:14-18, Mat 24:31, 1 Cor 15:51-52).
v. To call the people of Israel together so that the camp could move on, (Num 10:2).
vi. To announce the dedication of the temple, (2 Chr 5:12-13).
vii. To announce the Day of Atonement, Lev 25:9 and feast days (Num 10:10).
x. To announce the start of battles and feast days, (Num 10:9-10).

---

[147] Ibid., 25.

xi. To announce the arrival of the Ark of the Covenant into Jerusalem, (1 Chr 15:24).

xii. To announce disaster upon Israel because of sin, (Isa 58:1, Jer 4:4-6, Jer 6:1,16-19, 51:25-29, Eze 33:1-8, Hosea 7:16, 8:1, Amos 3:60).

xiii. To announce the warnings of God to the world, (Rev 1:10).

The point in each is that God is about to judge His people or the nations of the world. After setting forth the judgment of God on His people, John sets forth the judgment of the world by following the seven trumpets with the sharp sickle in God's hand, then with the angels with the seven bowls of God's wrath, then the judgment of the whore, the judgment of the beast, the judgment of Babylon, the judgment of the false prophet (the last great confederacy of evil), the judgment on the dragon, and the judgment on death itself. Each scene of judgment has a greater intensity than what went before. This suggests that the judgment of God, as severe as it might be, it contains mercy or what is called a certain sense of provisionality. Of course, the provisionality needs not be taken to mean that there is no finality. When God acts, each action has finality. The purpose of the great eschatological judgment is to bring the finality to all actions of judgment that have gone before. The judgment is to be as absolute for the rebellious as it has been for the righteous. "No Supreme Court of the future will have superior jurisdiction or be able to question what has taken place in God's court."[148] The judgment against evil is not reversible. The last enemy that shall be destroyed is death (1 Cor 15:51). "Death and Hades were thrown into the lake of fire" (Rev 20:14). This in a way brings about silence, not just in heaven for half an hour, but silence in hell for the ceaseless ages of eternity. I now restate in a chronological order the detail of judgment as it arises from Revelation 8 and the following chapters.

---

[148] Ibid., 26.

Judgment with the seven trumpets

Following the seals that deal with the situation of the saints (Rev 6,7), the seven trumpets are presented (Rev 8:2-11). They are basically modeled after the plagues against Egypt. In using the plagues as his model John points to the final disasters that are to afflict the world. At the beginning of the experience, God's word to Pharaoh through Moses was, "let my people go that they may worship me"(Ex 8:1), but Pharaoh refused and the plagues resulted. So the messages of the trumpets will carry the word of warning and the word of judgment for the world. Revelation 8:7 through 11:19 note that:

a. The first trumpet is blown and hail and fire are thrown onto the earth. A third of the earth, a third of the trees and all the grass are burnt up (8: 7).

b. The second trumpet is blown and something like a great mountain with fire is thrown into the sea, and the sea becomes blood. A third of the living creatures on the sea die and a third of the ships are destroyed (8: 8, 9).

c. The third trumpet is blown and a great star falls from heaven on a third of the rivers and the water springs, and a third of the waters become bitter (8: 10).

d. The fourth trumpet is blown and plunges a third of the sun, a third of the stars and a third of the day and the night into utter darkness (8: 12).

e. The fifth trumpet is blown and the first of three grcat woes begins as the sun and the earth are darkened with smoke from the shaft of the bottomless pit. Coming from the midst of the smoke are amalgamated horse-like locusts which are given the authority of scorpions to sting and torment those people who do not have the seal of God on their foreheads (9:1-11).

f. The sixth trumpet is blown and four angels who had been bound at the Euphrates are released, and with their troops of cavalry they are given power to kill a third of humankind with fire, smoke and sulfur which come out of the horses' mouths (9: 13-19).

g. The seventh trumpet is blown and there is a returning to the order of heavenly worship, with loud voices in heaven giving glory to God. But the worship order is not in its completeness, as the judgment is still to be consummated when God's temple opens in heaven and His covenant is seen within the temple. From the temple issue flashes of lightning, rumblings, thunders, an earthquake and heavy hail (11:15-19).

The trumpets are warnings to the world because they only affect a third of humankind. Despite the disasters that they bring upon the world, humanity refuses to repent and hence the witness of God, through the voice of His church, His angels and His holy prophets (Rev 10-14) occur as an interlude between the sixth and the seventh trumpet. When they have finished their witness, the seventh trumpet ushers in the end of the world. Thus the kingdom of the world becomes the kingdom of Christ and there is the final act of judgment (Rev 11:15-19).

Judgment at the winepress of the divine wrath

John moves beyond the Egyptian plagues and the temple imagery to use one of his great agricultural illustrations to emphasize God's final actions of the judgment. He states that two angels with sharp sickles are commanded by the one seated on the throne to trust in their sickles to reap the harvests of the earth (Rev 14:14-16). The Son of Man and an angel will reap the harvest of the fruits that are ripe or fit to meet their Lord. Another angel is told by the Son of Man to swing his sickle over the earth to gather the vintage of the earth for the winepress of God's wrath (Rev 14:17-20). This brings reminders of the many parables of separation told by Jesus and recorded by Matthew. In the parable of the "wheat" and "darnel," for example, the wheat, that represents the true children of God who are being preserved for the eternal kingdom, is gathered at last for the granary. The darnel, which represents the children of the evil one, will be pulled up and cast into the fiery furnace of the divine wrath, "where there will be weeping and gnashing of teeth" (Matt 13:24-30, 36-43). There is also the parable of the seine net in which the good fish are kept for the kingdom of God, while the bad fish are thrown away into the fiery furnace (Matt 13:47-50). There is the parable of the ten virgins, in which the wise go with the bridegroom to the wedding while the foolish are locked out (Matt 25:1-13). And there is also the parable of the sheep and goats. In this parable the Son of Man will put the sheep on His right hand, readied for the life of the kingdom, while the goats are to be placed on His left hand, readied for eternal punishment (Matt 25:31-46). In every illustration one might note that all provisional judgments must stand under the ultimate judgment of God. His judgment is final and is above every human judgment.[149]

This theme of the separation of "the righteous" from "the wicked," "the children of light" from "the children of darkness," and those who keep the commandments of God and receive His seal from those who worship the beast and his image and receive his mark, is very emphatic in John. He presses it to a final conclusion in the issue of the great harvest. Here the blood of the wicked will flow from God's winepress (Rev 14:14-20), thus indicating that God does not regard with impunity those who have broken His will.[150] As Karl Barth says, God is the Primary Lawgiver. He is Himself the *Lex*. He is the Source and Limit of all *leges.*[151] The central point John makes is that God is the revealer of all true laws and that He will bring judgment against anyone who rejects the word of his command. He sends the sickle of the divine mercy to save the righteous and the sickle of the divine wrath to bring destruction on all those who profane the name of the divine and challenge the rule of His throne. In the

---

[149] Reinhold Niebuhr (1974), Justice and Mercy, edited by Ursula M. Niebuhr (New York: Harper and Row), 55-56.
[150] Ibid., 49.
[151] Karl Barth (1956), Church Dogmatics IV:I The Doctrine of Reconciliation (Edinburgh: T & T Clark),
530-531.

words of the modern battle hymn written by Julia Ward Howe (1861):

> Mine eyes have seen the glory of the coming of the Lord;
> He is trampling out the vintage where the grapes of wrath are stored;
> He has loosed the fateful lightning of His terrible swift sword;
> His truth is marching on.

The work of judgment and the work of mercy go along together. God in His love and kindness brings the judgment but holds his hands, for repentance. But in a final act he will bring it all together.

Judgment with the seven last plagues

From the imagery of the sickle, John returns to the imagery of the Egyptian plagues. Egypt and Babylon are, for John, the historical symbols of greatest opposition for God's people. John notes, therefore, that as it happened in Egypt, so now it happens at the end to Roman/Babylon:

a. The first angel pours his bowl on the earth, and foul and painful sores come on those who have the mark of the beast and on those who worship its image (Rev 16:2).

b. The second angel pours out his bowl on the sea. It becomes like the blood of a corpse, and every living thing in the sea dies. (v. 3).

c. The third angel pours out his bowl into the rivers and the springs of water. They become like blood (v. 4).

d. The fourth angel pours out his bowl on the sun. The wicked are scorched severely and curse God but do not repent and give Him glory (vv. 8-9).

e. The fifth angel pours his bowl on the throne of the beast, and its kingdoms are plunged in darkness. People gnaw their tongues and curse the God of heaven because of their pain and sores, but they do not repent of their deeds. They die while cursing God (vv. 10-11).

f. The sixth angel pours out his bowl on the river Euphrates. Its waters dry up, and the kings of the earth prepare themselves for a great and final conflagration, called in the Hebrew ***Harmageddon***. (vv. 12-16).

g. The seventh angel pours out his bowl and loud voices in heaven proclaim, "It is finished." And there are thunderings, flashes of lightning, rumblings, a violent earthquake, hailstones falling from heaven on people who curse God for the plague of hail (vv. 17-20).

The trumpets and the bowls compared

	Trumpets	**Bowls**
First	Hail fire mixed with blood hurled to the earth, third of the earth, trees and green grass burned up.	Ugly and painful sours on those who had the mark of the beast and worship his image.
Second	Third of sea tuned to blood, third of creatures in the sea died, third of ships destroyed.	Sea tuned to blood, everything in the sea died.
Third	Third of waters turned bitter, many people died.	Rivers and springs became blood.
Fourth	A third of the day and night was without light.	Sun scorches people with fire.
Fifth	Locus out of the Abyss torture mankind for five months.	Kingdom plunged into darkness, men gnawed their tongues in agony.
Sixth	Third of mankind killed by fire, smoke and sulphur i.e. war.	Three evil spirits (frogs) gather kings of the earth for battle on the great day of God Almighty.
Seventh	End of the age, time o f the judgment, lightening, thunder, earthquake, hailstorm.	The end of the age, flashes of lightening, thunder, a great earthquake and plague of hail.

The bowls, the trumpets and the seals come in groups of four first, followed by a more severe group of three. The final act of judgment is decisive. William Barclay, thus, comments that "In this final series of terrors John seems to have gathered together the horrors from all the stories of the avenging wrath of God and have hurled them on the unbelieving world in one last terrible deluge of disaster."[152] During this moment the consciences of the wicked are awakened, and that which lies hidden in them is awakened, but they do not (no cannot) repent. They will only curse the name of God, and then in the end will turn to confess (like the saints) that God is just. This final confession is the issue that Satan has been trying to contest for the millennia, but now it is proven that Satan is wrong and God is in the right.

Judgment against the trinity of evil

The judgment thus turns on the confederacy of deception that is symbolized by the trinity of evil. These are the satanic agents that have carried on the satanic work through the millennia of history. They carry all the power resident in the false systems of religions and in the socio-political and economic systems of the world that is necessary to oppress the people of God (cf. Rev 13; 17). They act and speak blasphemously against God, against God's name, and against God's heavenly temple. When they find that their work is not effective against God they will turn against God's saints. They are ever ready to use words of persuasion and actions of harassment. And even though they suffer temporary judgments, and receive a "mortal wound," such a wound does not stop them in their display of arrogance against God and His saints (cf. Rev 13:3ff.).

More than 4000 years ago the Babylonian system built a tower at Babel and spoke arrogantly against God. God brought

---

[152] William Barclay (1976), The Revelation of John Vol. 2 (Philadelphia: The Westminster Press), 126.

judgment against it when He confused its language and scattered its people across the world with varied languages (Gen 11:1-9). But in every language today the voices of opposition continue. The Scriptural record about the historical behavior of Babylon is great. It is not my interest to recite it here. One can find a part of the record in Kings, Ezra, Esther, Psalms, Isaiah, Jeremiah, Ezekiel, Daniel, Micah, Zechariah, and Revelation. What they say is that Babylon has gone about in the world conquering, oppressing, and persecuting God's servants, corrupting God's truth, deceiving people, and blaspheming the name of God. In effect, Babylon is a persistent force of opposition against God. At every stage of history it has sought to re-form itself, but has carried forward it great objectives, that of blaspheming the name of God and destroying His people. In speaking to the nature of the Babylonian reform, Duane Watson says, "Babylon is symbolic of the power, influence, idolatry and wickedness of Rome. This was the position of the early Church and has remained the majority opinion" until today.[153] Other persons claim that Rome works with the same spirit of syncretization that was resident in the Babylonian system. Today such syncretization is reflected in an ecumenical frame. What is clear is that Roman/Babylon has made conquest after conquest and has led the world into opposition against God.

When the people of the world see that the beast, the whore, and Rome/Babylon have deceived them, they will turn against them (it) and all who work with them (it), leaving them (it) "desolate" (Rev 17). The voices of the wicked will be calling for the punishment of the deceptive powers with plagues, death, mourning and famine, while the saints will ask God to make this punishment double (Rev 19:1-3). The judgments come and finally the powers are called to confront the lake of fire that burns with sulfur ((Rev 20:4,10). The announcement of their fall is rightly stated in the "loud voice" of an angel (Rev 18: 1-2; cf. 14:8),

---

[153] Duane Watson (1992), "Babylon," The Anchor Bible Dictionary (New York: Doubleday), 563-566.

because they have made all nations "to drink of the wine of its fornication"(18:3).

In the divine judgment God will attack Great Babylon with the same fury with which it has attacked the saints of God. Saints and sinners alike lament its fall, but for two different reasons. The saints lament and rejoice because they are satisfied that their cry for justice has been answered by God (18:1-9). In their spiritual pilgrimage the two primary poles of speech available to them are praise and lament. They lament when they see their fellow servants falling by the way. Often enough along the path of their lives they are reduced to silence. But their silent lament is put away when God deals with the alien powers that oppress them. Any sound from the saints is a welcome sound, because it says that the saints have regained a voice to cry to God. In the end of the age the saints will not lament so much as they will rejoice for their salvation from the condemnation of those who wish their destruction (18: 20-24).[154]

The lament of the wicked (the kings, the merchants and all that have done business with Babylon) is not so much because of any sadness for their lostness or because of any sorrow for Babylon but because at the end they cannot practice with her the idolatrous business that was so dear to them (18:9-19).[155] Their lament as quoted by John is gathered from the Old Testament, especially from within the books of Isaiah and Jeremiah. I quote a part of the last of the great lament, which John gathers from Isaiah and Jeremiah:

> With such violence Babylon the great city will be thrown down, and will be found no more; and the sound of harpists and minstrels and of flutists and trumpeters will be heard in you no more; and an artisan of any trade will be found in

---

[154] Stephen E. Fowl (1997), The Theological Interpretation of Scripture (Cambridge, MA: Blackwell), 208.

[155] Leon Morris (1987), Revelation: Tyndale New Testament Commentaries, (Grand Rapids, MI: Wm. B. Eerdmans), 215-217.

you no more; and the sound of the millstone will be heard in you no more; and the light of a lamp will shine in you no more; and the voice of bridegroom and bride will be heard in you no more; for your merchants were the magnates of the earth, and all nations were deceived by your sorcery. And in you was found the blood of the prophets and of the saints, and of all that have been slaughtered on earth (Rev 18:21-24; cf. Isa 42:2f; Jer 51: 63f).

The prophet Isaiah had said:

The Lord has broken the staff of the wicked, the scepter of rulers which is used to strike the peoples in fury with unceasing strokes, which subdued the nations in anger with unrestrained persecution. The whole earth is at rest and is quiet; they break forth into shouts of joy. Even the cypress trees rejoice over you, and the cedars of Lebanon, saying, 'since you were laid low, no tree cutter comes up against us. Sheol from beneath is excited over you to meet you when you come; it arouses for you the spirits of the dead, all the leaders of the earth; it raises all the kings of the nations from their thrones.' "They will all respond and say to you, 'Even you have been made weak as we, you have become like us. Your pomp and the music of your harps have been brought down to Sheol; maggots are spread out as your bed beneath you, and worms are your covering.' How have you fallen from heaven, O star of the morning, and son of the dawn! You have been cut down to the earth, you who have weakened the nations! But you said in your heart," 'I will ascend to heaven; I will raise my throne above the stars of God, and I will sit on the mount of assembly in the recesses of the north. I will ascend above the heights of the clouds; I will make myself like the Most High.' "Nevertheless you will be thrust down to Sheol, to the recesses of the pit. Those who see you will gaze at you, they will ponder over you, saying, 'Is this the man who made the earth tremble, who shook kingdoms, who made the world like a wilderness and overthrew its cities, who did not allow prisoners to go home?' All the kings of the nations lie in glory, each in his own tomb. But you have been cast out of your tomb like a rejected branch, clothed with the slain who are pierced with a sword who go down to the stones of the pit, like a trampled corpse. You will not be united with them in burial, because you have ruined your country, you have slain your people. May the offspring of evildoers not be mentioned forever. Prepare for his sons a place of slaughter because of the iniquity of their fathers. They must not arise and take possession of the earth and fill the face of the world with cities. 'And I will rise up against them,' declares the Lord of hosts, 'and will cut them off,' declares the Lord. 'I will also make it a possession for the hedgehog, and swamps of water, and I will sweep it with the broom of destruction,' declares the Lord of hosts (Isaiah 14: 4-23) (NASB).

And Jeremiah had lamented:

Summon many against Babylon, all those who bend the bow: encamp against her on every side, let there be no escape. Repay her according to her work; according to all that she has done, so do to her; for she has become arrogant against the Lord, against the Holy One of Israel. Therefore her young men will fall in her streets, and all her men of war will be silenced in that day declares the Lord. 'Behold, I am against you, O arrogant one,' declared the Lord God of hosts, 'for your day has come, the time when I shall punish you. And the arrogant one will stumble and fall with no one to raise him up; and I shall set fire to his cities, and it will devour all his environs' (Jerm. 50:29-32) (NASB).

> Lift up a signal in the land; blow a trumpet among the nations! Consecrate the nations against her, summon against her the kingdoms of Ararat, Minni and Ashkenaz; appoint a marshal against her, bring up the horses like bristly locusts.
> Consecrate the nations against her, the kings of the Medes, their governors and all their prefects, and every land of their dominion. So the land quakes and writhes, for the purposes of the Lord against Babylon stand, to make the land of Babylon desolation without inhabitants. The mighty men of Babylon have ceased fighting, they stay in the strongholds; their strength is exhausted, they are becoming like women; their dwelling places are set on fire, the bars of her gates are broken. One courier runs to meet another, and one messenger to meet another, to tell the king of Babylon that his city has been captured from end to end; the fords also have been seized, and they have burned the marshes with fire, and the men of war are terrified. For thus says the Lord of hosts, the God of Israel: 'The daughter of Babylon is like a threshing floor at the time it is stamped firm; yet in a little while the time of harvest will come for her' (Jerm 51:27-33) (NASB).

In effect, from the latter trajectory, the festal music of self-gratification and self-exaltation stops as Babylon and all the (cities and) centers of opposition turn to the true God and confess His justice. The arrogance of the wicked has come to God's ears. (Isa 52:29). Their unkindly attitudes toward the people of God are stopped (Isa 52:24). The penultimate act of the judgment against the corporate systems of wickedness has taken place. Babylon, the city of Babel--"The gate of the gods" has fallen. The center of confusion and every "foul spirit" will be no more. The climatic act of judgment must still take place. It must silence the dragon and all the demons that have challenged God concerning God's reality and right to speak (Lk 8:31).

Judgment on the Dragon

The dragon speaks, he spoke in heaven, and he spoke in Eden and has been speaking for the millennia of earth's history. He argues well, as one poet says, that it is better to be a ruler in hell than a servant in heaven. When he speaks, he ever seeks to usurp the place of God. It is therefore a necessary fact that he must be silenced (Rev 12:9; 20:10,14). When he presented his phenomena of enchantments of magic though the serpent in Eden, he spoke with much cunning. And the question he posed remains the fundamental basis on which he challenges the sovereignty of God, even today. "Did God say, 'you shall not eat of any tree in the garden'?" The simplest reading of the question shows that he intended to cast doubt on the word of God. A deeper reading shows that he intended to change God's word. By the doubt he introduced, and the change of the word, he drew Eve into his confidence. He offered her the three great promises he would use for the millennia to corrupt all human relations to God, namely: (1) that humanity would be like God, (2) that humanity would have absolute wisdom, knowing good and evil, and (3) that humanity would not die (Gen 3). Whatever more one might say of this, it is clear that Satan made the point that "God's word is not to be trusted." In Daniel and Revelation, it is noted that he not only works though serpents, but that he works through individual human beings and governmental agencies to speak haughty and blasphemous words against the Most High God (Dan 7:25, Rev 13:5). In Revelation 16:13 John describes him as working through the perfect confederacy of the trinity of evil, a trinity that seeks to usurp the divine Trinity. It says:

> And I saw three foul spirits like frogs coming from the mouth of the dragon, from the mouth of the beast, and from the mouth of the false prophet. These are demonic spirits, performing signs, which go abroad to the kings of the

> whole world, to assemble them to the great day of God the Almighty (Rev 16:13, 14).

Until his final arrest this dragon voice will work through every incarnation of evil to carry out his magic spell upon all human kind.[156] Since it would take a long study to present a detail of his activity, I have created a ten point summary outline to show the fundamental intention behind his deceptive speeches in history.

1. The Dragon speaks to challenge the very existence of God

More fundamental than the more simple interpretations I gave above concerning the dragon's speech in Eden, is the fact that the dragon has always intended to displace God from the world and set up a world government. But let us deal here with the question of the displacement of God. The beginning of the Bible reads, "In the beginning God created the heaven and the earth." Then there is great emphasis on the power of God's creative word. In the first temptation this dragon sought to challenge this creative word in the question, "Did God say?" While the intellectual crisis of belief in God as spoken of in our culture might not seem to have been present, the point of the temptation was to challenge the supremacy of God. There was a movement then from what we know today as monotheism to polytheism, and from polytheism to paganism, and from paganism to skepticism, and from skepticism to gnosticism, and from gnosticism to agnosticism, and from agnosticism to atheism, and from atheism to deism, and from deism to pantheism and pan-entheism. It was not a movement as some evolutionary anthropologists have suggested a movement from animism, to polytheism, to pantheism and so on, until humanity discovered monotheism. Whatever the strategy, from the beginning, it has been the dragon's greatest pleasure to confuse and suppress belief in God. Many in our world still support what

---

[156] Marian Berry (1990), Warning (Brushton, New York: TEACH Services).

Robert Ingersol said a number of years ago, namely that "Our ignorance is God." "Man is the highest intelligence in the world.[157] More contemporarily some persons say, "God is a meaningless sound." "God suffers from a terminal case of internal incoherency, contradictions and absurdities." In effect, "God does not exist."

The dragon has spoken in his dark counsel to confuse the minds of humanity in the earth. His interpretations of the signs in nature, in his séances, in his performance of miracles, and through his religious, philosophical and scientific discourses, he seeks to destroy the world.[158] It is always the concern of the Scripture that while a diversity of voices are heard in the earth, that the people of God must have a clear sense of discerning so that they will not be duped. This is why the warning of Scripture is given that not everyone who has said, "Lord, Lord," is a voice from God.[159]

2. The Dragon has been trying to destroy the government of God

The second foundational issue in the dragon's speech in Eden was to raise questions about God's character and government. First, he raised questions about the divine existence, and then he challenged the right of God to govern the earth. Extensions of his question, "Did God say?" would read, "If God exists, what kind of God?" "Is God arbitrary?" "Is God vindictive, capricious, torturous, and unjust." "Is God, a God of love and mercy?" "What kind of God is God?" Each little question is very connected to the question, "Did God say?" And the rhetoric of the dragon has been very powerful since Eden. "If God is merciful," he says, "God cannot be just." "If God is love, God cannot be

---

[157] Robert Ingersol (1990), On the Gods and Other Essays (Buffalo, New York: Prometheus Books), 39

[158] Norman Gulley (1998), Christ is Coming, (Hagerstown, MD: Review and Herald).

[159] See Author Peacocke (1986), God and the New Biology (San Francisco: Harper and Row) Note especially the chapter, "Man, God and Evolution: Yesterday."

righteous, and so on." He attributed the death of all beings to God. The floods, the wars, the famines, are all referred to today as "acts of God." From presenting the view that the Old Testament God is a God of wrath, while the New Testament God is a God of love, to the idea that the judgment is something to fear, the dragon began his work in Eden to fill the minds of human beings with doubts so profound that many have lost good reason for worshiping God. Paul puts it precisely, "For though they knew God, they did not honor him as God or give thanks to him. . ." (Rom 1:21). Thus the root of the attack upon the divine government is being by many agents. I am indebted to an author with whom I have not always agreed for the following outline of the dragon's intonations against God's word. He argues that the dragon says:

God has given a law that His subjects cannot obey, therefore God is cruel.
God has given a law that His subjects cannot obey, therefore God is selfish.
God has given a law that His subjects cannot obey, therefore God is stern.
God has given a law that His subjects cannot obey, therefore God is severe.
God has given a law that His subjects cannot obey, therefore God is arbitrary.
God has given a law that His subjects cannot obey, therefore God is unforgiving.
God has given a law that His subjects cannot obey, therefore God is satanic.
God has given a law that His subjects cannot obey, therefore His character is faulty.
God has given a law that His subjects cannot obey, therefore He is lacking wisdom.

God has given a law that His subjects cannot obey, therefore he is lacking in love.[160]

What the dragon urged upon the creatures of heaven and still urges upon our world, is that changes in the laws of heaven are necessary for there to be stability in God's government.[161] The dragon insists that every law of heaven is "up for grabs"; from those that urge against idolatry, to those that govern worship of the true and Living God, to those that call for a true Seventh-day Sabbath rest, to those that govern the family and the home, to those that call for kindness to each other, to those that speak against selfishness and covetousness, every law that is of God must be abolished. In which case humanity can establish its own order of authority, show forth the special circumstances in which the divine laws are to be obeyed, make selfishness commendable, formulate its own kind of justice and devise its own sort of ethical and moral systems (Hos 4:6). In effect, the dragon pushes a non-Theistic morality

Revelation 13-17 portrays the earthly governmental systems that are offered their power by the dragon. Their lust for power, their defense of the immoral practices of war and genocide, their historical adoption of systems of feudalism, fascism, utilitarianism, nationalism, racism, ethnocentrism, tribalism, and hatred of all sorts, are recorded in Scripture, and one needs not doubt that all of these activities are to reach their end when the dragon is silenced.

3. The Dragon has been trying to silence God by presenting himself as Christ.

A third issue connected with the dragon's challenge to the existence of God is the dragon's attack against Christ. Christ, as

---

[160] Ralph Larson (1998), The Hellish Torch (Printed in the United States of America).

[161] Norman Gulley (1998), Christ is Coming (Hagerstown, MD: Review and Herald), 326-327.

the Word of God, has been ever under attack. He was attacked in heaven (Rev 12:3). He was attacked at His birth (Rev 12:5). He has been attacked throughout earth's history (Rev 12:7-11). Now in the final crisis of history, He is being attacked in His Church (Rev 12:17). Maybe the greatest contradiction of history is that the Church that is to teach the story of Christ has served as the agent of the greatest attack. Hans Kung has given a rather extensive commentary of a syncretistic culture which seeks to silence Christ when he says that Christ has been turned into a principle, a dogma, a pietistic image, a revolutionary, an ideology, a Christ of dream, and so on, but there is no real Christ to speak as the Word of God.[162]

It is common knowledge that the Christ of the church has been silenced through the historical debates on the nature of Christ.[163] And there have been the silencing of Christ through the Jesus of history debates that have produced Jesusology.[164] On the contemporary plain, there are productions of an evolutionary Christ, which seeks to destroy the reality of the Crucified and Coming One. Taking his lead from Pierre Teilhard de Chardin, Leonardo Boff, and some other theologians of his thinking, have reached a great point of Christological trivialization when they say that the Christian view of Christ is Cosmogenesis, which gives rise to biogenesis, and anthropogenesis which emerges from biogenesis, and from anthropogenesis Christogenesis has emerged. This evolutionary Christ, they argue, is a major breakthrough in the

---

[162] Hans Kung (1978), On Being a Christian, translated by Edward Quinn (New York: Doubleday), 128-174.

[163] Both Jon Sobino (1976), in Christology at the Crossroads, and Leonardo Boff (1978), in Jesus Christ Liberator argue that the history which brought forth the Christological dogmas of the centuries have been produced from "word, silence and faltering speech." No wonder that there has been so much confusion in the debates.

[164] I first found this term in Leonardo Boff's Jesus Christ Liberator, where he makes the point that the history of Jesus has been debated for a century and has made the God who speaks to us in Jesus Christ quite remote to us.

eyes of Christian faith.[165] The Christs of the New Age Movement, the Christ of the pagan spiritualistic movements of religion and the Christ of contemporary science are the ultimate synthesis of the evolutionary Christ. He has been silenced through many false claims and impersonations.[166] But I conclude that the claimants may go from East to West and North to South making their idolatrous claims, but what is clear in their presentations is that they are part of the confederacy, which creates the antichrist.

The antichrist portrayed in Scripture is an antichristian character (1 Jn 2:18) that tries to present himself as Christ. He has worked in religious and secular systems. Moreover, he operates through personal and impersonal agents, through individuals and groups of people, and through leaders and nations. He has had many forerunners, has cast many shadows, (1 Jn 2:18; 4:3) but is always the pure and unalloyed devil (cf. 2 Jn 1:7), who is the universal enemy of God and his covenant people (Eph 6: 11,12). As a "loud mouth" he hides behind a mask of goodness and deception, and when he fails to get his way he will seek to destroy the saints of God. I shall return later to the picture of the "transfigured devil." For now I note what John says of his last effort to destroy the saints: "Then the dragon was angry with the woman, and went to make war with the rest of her children, those who keep the commandments of God and hold the testimony of Jesus" (Rev 12:17).

---

165 Leonardo Boff (1978), Jesus Christ Liberator, (New York: Obris), 234.

166 Roger Schmidt says that the hope that a messianic figure will come to establish a new, righteous age is very popular in the world cultures. Situations in which believers have identified a particular person as Messiah or proclaimed that the time was at hand for the Messiah's return have been many. But most predictions have ended with disappointment, and thus have resulted in the repudiation of the belief. cf. Roger Schmidt, Exploring Religion (1988 edition) (Belmont, Calif: Wadsworth), 156-157. Though messianic faith has persisted throughout the world, there is a general cynicism concerning Him who says He is the authentic Messiah (cf. Matt 24:24; 2 Pet 3:3).

4. The Dragon uses pressure and persecution to silence the saints of God.

In expanding on the point concerning the dragon's attack upon the church, which was noted in Revelation 12:17, it is to be said that his voice is most powerful when he accuses the saints. The history of the saints under attack can be found in many history books, but In a review of the book of Daniel it can be shown how the Satanic attacks develops. In the first chapter king Nebuchadnezzer changes the food, the names and the education of the Hebrew worthies to get them to reject the laws of their God. This is followed in the third chapter when the king uses loud music to persuade the worthies to reject God. Under the pressure of the loud music the king hopes that he could confuse the minds of the worthies to turn to idolatry. It is a repeat of the dragon's strategy in Eden. When the music does not bring the desired persuasion to the Hebrew worthies, the worthies are threatened with the fire of death. In chapter six, the threat is brought upon the leader of the group of the worthies. Daniel is thus watched by a hundred and nineteen satraps and threatened with the lion's den if he is to pray to the God of heaven. In chapter seven the dragon challenges God, even in judgment, by speaking arrogantly against the throne. The remainder of the book paints a picture of the open upon God's throne. Every form of accusation and destruction is employed for a "final solution." The record shows that from Old Testament times in the captivity of the covenant people through New Testament times, in the crucifixion of Jesus Christ, there is one direction that the dragon leads – confusion, pressure, persecution, and death. He had not let up on his strategy in the dark days of the Roman Empire and the Middle Ages. Nor did he forget during the times of the Inquisition, the Holocaust in Europe, or the Baxter rebellion in China or in the many other unnamed times of trial that he has brought upon the people of God. Nor does he fail to remember in these last moments of earth's history, for it is at these times that his effort can be most intense. It is now that the people of God are open to confrontation (cf. Rev 16:2-6; Matt 24:9-13). Every attack will severely test the faith of the saints, but everyone who will be saved will hold on to the promises of God (cf. Rev 1:9; 6:9; Heb 10:33).

5. The Dragon creates distrust of the Scripture to silence God

In order to convince religious persons, even "so called Christians," that he is the Lord of the earth, the Dragon makes every effort to discredit the word of Scripture. "Did God say?" This has been the historical question. He has made it appear that the God of Scripture has not spoken, or that we cannot be sure what He has said. He makes it seem that many things in the Scripture are incredible. He points to the fact that some things in the Scripture are not scientifically accurate. He thus gets people to change or abandon many parts of the Scripture. Then he adds his own thoughts and words. John warns against such attacks upon the Scripture when he notes that there are those who try to "take away from" or "add to" the prophetic word (Rev 22:18, 19 cf. Matt 16:3; Lk 12:56; 1 Cor 14:26; 2 Pet 1:20).

The dragon boasts that the authority has been given to him through profound historical church traditions or new philosophical and analytical strategies for Scriptural interpretations. He has argued for special understanding of the Scripture for many millennia. Then he uses superstitions and obscurantism to make it seem that he is the reservoir of truth. In an effort to introduce His oppressive principles, he agues that Scripture is silent on certain questions (Rev 3:17; Matt 23:24; 2 Pet 1:9). Through some contemporary interpreters he calls for a "hermeneutic of suspicion" instead of a "hermeneutic of faith." From his perspective he offers a need to deconstruct and reconstruct bits of truths that he wishes to introduce as biblical truths. But Eta Linnemann tells us that such methods of interpretation are not so much the result of scientific investigation as they are the result of prejudice.[167] When people even use any appeal to the silence of the Bible to sustain their practices of evil, one has to understand that it is the dragon that is leading them away from the truth. While God says, "Listen to me" (cf. Isa 51:1, 4, 7; 55:2), the dragon makes a lot of so called intellectual noises, in addition to his silent propaganda in order that the people of the world might not hear any word from God (cf. Jer 7:26).

A word of caution that I use for a conclusion on this point of discussion is that as we look to the future we must be aware that the dragon will have much theological reflection and pay more attention to philosophy and many areas in science and the sociology of knowledge than to Bible truth. Our task must be to encourage people to stay humbly by the word. Do not put doubt on God's word. Listen to God's word. Do not change God's word. Test every word that claims to be from God.

6. The Dragon uses the silence of conscience to silence the voice of God

The dragon is a master-worker at making people spiritually deaf so that they cannot hear the voice of God. "Did God say?" He makes them disdain the warnings of God's word. He wears away their consciences – that is the God factor with which they were born, so that they may not be able to recognize the voice of God. When the Spirit of God appeals to all who have ears to listen (Rev 2:7, 11, 17, 29; 3:6, 13, 22), Satan blocks up their ears with many false suggestions (cf. Zech 3:1; Matt 4:10). He fills the mind with darkened thoughts and prideful practices in order to challenge the divine power (Rev 3:17; Jn 9:40). God, therefore, lodges a legitimate complaint against disobedient people when He says

[167] Eta Linnemann (1990), Historical Criticism of the Bible: Methodology or Ideology: Reflections of a Bultmannian Turned Evangelical, translated by Robert W. Yarbrough (Grand Rapids, MI.: Baker Book House).

through Jeremiah, "To whom shall I speak and give warning, that they may hear? See their ears are closed that they cannot listen. The word of the Lord is to them an object of scorn; they take no pleasure in it" (Jer 6:10). Through listening to themselves in what is called the Human Consciousness Movements, Satan makes every effort to spiritualize away the truth about God and to stop the ears of humanity. What Paul says in Romans has been at the heart of the great historical challenge, in the work of divine judgment, namely "For the wrath of God is revealed from heaven against all ungodliness and wickedness of those who by their wickedness suppress the truth . . . . For though they know God, they did not honor him as God or give thanks to him, but they became futile in their thinking, and their senseless minds were darkened. Claiming to be wise, they became fools, and they exchanged the glory of the immortal God for images resembling a mortal human being or birds or four-footed animals or reptiles. Therefore God gave them up in the lusts of their heats to impurity, to the degrading of their bodies among themselves, because they exchanged the truth about God for a lie and worshipped and served the creature rather then the Creator, who is blessed forever! Amen" (Rom 1:21-25). The contradictory note of life today is that in the midst of a growing spiritual revival there is also a high current of **secularism** in which God is being disposed of. The persistent voice of God in the heart is present, but the dragon tries to drown that voice through his secularizing effort.

7. The Dragon employs secular ideologies to aid his cause in silencing God

In effect, much of the satanic noise of the last days will be made through religious and para-religious movements, but he will also find great support in the secular and atheistic frame. It has always been Satan's studied strategy to attack the people of God from within the ranks of religion and from without. After the saints came through the religious persecutions of the Middle Ages and felt secure with the religious fervor of the Reformation, the dragon attacked the saints with ideas of the Enlightenment. "Did God say?" The derisive voices that spoke through Voltaire, Spencer, Feuerbach, Marx, Freud, Nietzsche, Ingersol, Russell, and so on, have allowed some saints to take secular methodologies to interpret theology. The result of the effort has been the assertions that "God is dead," "God is absent" from the world and so on. Today the world is reaping the harvest of the seeds sown through the secularistic movements such as nihilism, communism, humanism, materialism, consumerism, hedonism, objectivism, behaviorism, relativism and other secular arrangements. Although there is religious renewal in the world, it is competing with the secularizing effort.

What Paul Tillich noted many years ago is still upon us. "The whole field of man's spiritual life is [being] taken . . ."[168] Writing at the same time with Tillich, Martin Buber noted that that humanity was living between the time of God's absence and the time of his coming.[169] Tillich bluntly observed that the issue affecting life in his age was the fact that humanity had found many ways to be "self-sufficient." The understanding today is that the spirit of self-sufficiency has reached a greater height. In effect, if the scientific discoveries of the last century made humanity think that it had no need of God, we are more threatened today by our contemporary discoveries. God, it is being said, is only a God of the initial conditions. God fine-tuned the world that came about as a result of antropic coincidences, but now God has left the world to humanity to run it. And our temptation is to forget God in the desire to be our own bosses. With the view that science will lead the world to a better future, we need to see that God is out of the picture, totally. The tragic consequence of our time is that God has

---

[168] Paul Tillich (1959), Theology of Culture (New York: Oxford University Press), 7.

[169] Martin Buber (1957), Eclipse of God, (New York: Harper Tourch books), Read the chapter on "Religion and Modern Thinking."

been rejected as Creator or Offerer of eternal life.[170] Has the dragon succeeded, "Is God speaking today?" This is a question to be contemplated in a future discussion. The general observation from social scientists is that there is a renewal of religiousness in some parts of the world.

8. The Dragon promises immortality to humanity to silence God

The dragon's foremost lie in Eden will be his last – the promise of immortality: "You shall be as gods." "You shall not surely die." For the millennia of earth's history he has worked to make it seem that what God has promised is immortality in sin. Humanity can be divinized and immortalized in its present condition, through some kind of spiritualization or re-incarnation. In this frame, he presents death as a friend to be embraced "for the sake of attaining Godhood." He argues, "Death is like throwing away old clothes." "Death is an illusion." He has connected the most pagan of ideas -- immortality of the soul -- with Christian and other religious thought. He uses ideas from Eastern religious thought such as reincarnation, or consciousness in death, and has popularized them in the world that is so desperate to find immortality. He wants the world to think that he is the "author" and "finisher" of life.

As often as opportunity allows, the dragon portrays God as the author of devastations such as floods, earthquakes, storms, hurricanes, and diseases of every kind and death. In this way he has gotten the majority of humanity to hate God (Rev 8:5; 16:18; Matt 24:7). Thus when philosopher/theologian Anthony Flew focuses on the sufferings of children, then argues that, morally and logically, God does not love us,[171] he is a participant in the satanic effort to misrepresent God.

---

[170] Paul Tillich (1956), The Religious Situation, translated by H. Richard Niebuhr, (New York: World Publishing Co).
[171] Flew Anthony and Alisdar MacIntyre, general editors (1955), New Essays in Philosophical Theology, (New York: Macmillan), 98-99.

9. The Dragon seeks to deny the reality of his own existence

The idea behind the Edenic phenomena has been that the dragon is only a myth of history (Gen 3). As the serpent sheds it clothes, so the dragon has gotten many philosophers and theologians and practical religionists to argue away the reality of his existence. He has tried to argue away God's existence, and now it is his existence that is to be argued away. The idea that a dragon, Satan, demon or a devil might be just a left over of an underdeveloped part of the human evolution, is quite popular. He has gotten people to say that those who do wrong are simply not living up to their full potential for right. He has gotten them to say that human beings are submitting to some supernatural, alien forces of evil, for which they are not responsible. When the above alibis do not work, he argues otherwise, namely that there is something in the human psyche that is inspiring the forces of evil that cannot be explained. In this direction he has used the movies and novels and all of the public media to suggest that evil is just the work of imagination and artful creation. [172]

He even argues that hell is to be thought of as a metaphor instead of a reality.[173] Through the creation of a second chance place such as the Catholic idea of purgatory or other places of psychic consciousness,s supported by other religious systems, or by building a doctrine of universal salvation, or by arguing away the fall as a biblical idea, Satan has been able to dispose of the reality of hell. "What does God have to do with hell?" Satan asks. And without any effort to wait for a response, he turns the minds of humanity away from God. In the final moment of history the dragon will get his due for scripture says that the one who deceives

---

[172] Peter Vardy (1992), The Puzzle of Evil (Great Britain: Harper Collins), Chapter 14.
[173] Ibid.

the world will be thrown into the lake of fire and sulphur where the beast and the false prophets are (Rev 20:10).

10. The Dragon will transfigure himself into an angel of light to silence God

Before his voice is silenced forever, he carries forward his final deception. I refer to this the transfiguration of the dragon. He transfigures himself "into an angel of light" (2 Cor 11:14). The point was made that he has shed his clothes many times in history and will do it in his last ditch effort to deceive the world (Rev 20:8). He fell from heaven like a flash of lightning (Lk 10:18) and up to the end will present himself as burnished light. In this way, if it were possible he would deceive the elect into thinking that he is the true savior and ruler of the world. His penultimate word will be to call God a liar. Then he will be able to offer his final charm to humanity. Up to the end he presses the question upon the saints, as he pressed it at the crucifixion: "If God is that powerful, why does he not intervene in your case?" "If God is omnipotent, omniscient, and all loving, why does God not find time for his children confronting the plagues?" If effect, "If there is someone to be glorified, who is it?" "Why not the great miracle worker?" To place the story of the transfiguration of the dragon in bold relief let me precise it in the following way:

Satan presents himself as the creator of life.
God is thus presented as the creator of death.
Satan presents himself as the merciful friend.
God is presented as a mercurial, ill-tempered deity.
Satan presents himself as the author of tranquility and deliverance.
God is presented as the author of disease and destruction.
Satan presents himself as the omnipotent one.

God is presented as the impotent one.
Satan presents himself as the author of love and a worker of miracles.
God is presented as the author of suffering.
Satan presents himself as the justifier.
He presents God as the cruel judge and punisher.

The effort to usurp the place of God (Isa 14:4) has been a long and hard struggle (Rev 12:1). After loosing his battle with Michael in heaven, the dragon is cast out into the earth where he turns with complete venom against God and God's people. John says it well, that the dragon pours water out of his mouth against the woman, tries to destroy her son, and makes war with the remnant of her seed (Rev 12:1-17). John also notes how the dragon works with a mask of deception by speaking through the beast with seven heads and ten horns (Rev 13:1-4), and through the lamb-like beast (Rev 13:11). It also speaks through other strange creatures such as frogs (Rev 16:13,14). But the greatest part of its deception is where it tries to mimic the miracle working power of God and tries to gain the attention of the world through excitement (Rev 13:13-15; 16:14). When God determines that the dragon's game is to be stopped, God will break out of His silence to make it known that all of the noise has been unsubstantial. God will make it known that the great influence of the dragon in the earth has been only an illusion (Rev18:1-20:10).

Dragons have been in mythology and legend for thousands of years. Their stories have been inserted into nearly every world culture. In ancient Greece and Rome, they were thought to be connected with the Zodiac and with the gods, Zeus and Jupiter. In ancient China images of dragons were used to protect the palaces of kings, and the homes of the upper class. In all cultures where they are found, their general reflection is that of a composite animal infused with supernatural powers. In most cases they have tails filled with poisons and tongues and mouths spewing fierce fires. To bring into effect the greatest public consumption of dragons, they have been placed in art, flags, money, clothing, tattoos, automobiles, restaurants, taverns, adult and children films, and in many religious objects. A foremost point here is that in world history, the dragon has been, and is the most pompous, persistent, power of opposition against God. And whether he speaks in the silent symbols of world culture or with fiery words that are heard in every language of the earth, he speaks with the intent to attack and destroy the people of God and the name of God.

In commenting on how deceived and spiritually blinded the Scribes and Pharisees were, Jesus made a most explicit point when he said:

> You are from your father the devil, and you choose to do your father's desires. He was a murderer from the beginning and does not stand in truth, because there is no truth in him. When he lies he speaks according to his own nature, for he is a liar and father of lies (John 8:44).

By the above it is to be understood that the fundamental reality of this world is that Satan fills the earth with lies, hatred, and murder. His nature is founded on lies. The idiom of his language is lies. He speaks lying oracles. He corrupts the nature of human beings so that they speak lies (Acts 5:3). His prophets speak lies. The images he sets forth for people to worship are teachers of lies. Everything he speaks and does is related to lie.[174] We have been making the point often in this discussion that, Satan/the Dragon lies and sows hatred and commits murders. And since he knows that God cannot lie, he opposes God and all who are Godly. But the great reality of the future is that God with stop the lie and the liar.

---

[174] Anyone who opposes truth is from the devil (Cf. 1 Jn 2:21; Acts 5:3; Rom 3:13)

Silence in heaven and the trivialization of God's judgment

The fact that God has sometimes kept silent during the progression of evil has been the dragon's greatest opportunity for creating millions and millions of lies about God's authorship of evil. The Psalmist says in one context, "Why do you boast, great man, of your evil? . . . You make plans to ruin others; your tongue is like a sharp razor. You are always investing lies. You love evil more than good, and falsehood more than truth. You love to hurt people with your words, you liar." (Psa 52:1, 2-4).

But one of these days there is to be a grand reversal. The one who has guided the course of history, sometimes in apparent weakness, will rise up in judgment against evil. The wicked trivializes God's silence. Peter says, "In the last days scoffers will come asking where is the promise of his coming," and indulging their own lusts (2 Pet 3:3). They will deliberately ignore the facts of the creation, the flood, the divine time-lines concerning "the Day of Judgment," and demonstrate that they have no respect for God. But Peter warns them, "The Lord is not slow concerning his promise as some think of slowness, but is patient with you, not wanting any to perish, but all to come to repentance. But the day of the Lord will come like a thief, and then the heavens will pass away with a loud noise, and the elements will be dissolved with fire, and the earth and everything that is done on it will be disclosed" (1 Pet 3:4-13). For Isaiah the trivializers are to know that:

> The day of the Lord is coming, cruel, with fury and burning anger, to make the land desolation; and He will exterminate its sinners from it. For the stars of heaven and their constellations will not flash forth their light; the sun will be dark when it rises, and the moon will not shed its light. Thus I will punish the world for its evil, and the wicked for their iniquity; I will also put an end to the arrogance of the proud, and abase the haughtiness of the ruthless. I will make mortal man scarcer than pure gold, and mankind than the gold of Ophir. Therefore I shall make the heavens tremble, and the earth will be shaken from its place at the fury of the Lord of hosts in the day of His burning anger. And it will be that like a hunted gazelle, or like sheep with none to gather them, they will each turn to his own people,

> and each one flees to his own land. Anyone who is found will be thrust through, and anyone who is captured will fall by the sword. Their little ones also will be dashed to pieces before their eyes; their houses will be plundered and their wives ravished (Isaiah 13:8-16) (NASB).

They, who have said "There is no God," and that "they are gods," will be confronted by a God who can no longer keep His quiet (cf. Isa 41:14). The God who seemed at times not to offer any resistance to the arrogance of humanity will come to war. He will come to cast down "the accuser of the brethren" (Rev 12:10).

Throughout the heavenly silence Satan has spoken with a loud voice, but in the final judgment, it is God whose voice will be like a trumpet. God, the One who has suffered our fate will rise up against the one who creates the suffering. Christ the Slain will become the Slayer, the Advocate will become the Executioner, the Lamb will become the Lion of the tribe of Judah, and the Savior will become the Warrior Christ. Christ who is usually seen in a robe of mercy is now clothed in a robe dipped in blood (Rev 19:13). As He blows His trumpet, pours out His vials, tramples the grapes, unleashes His sword against iniquity, and carries out the act of throwing death and Hades into the lake of fire, He is declared as the "Lord of all."

There will be a reversal. The silent or powerless Lord will be exalted. The boasters shall shut their mouths because of Him (Isa 52:15). He has issued the command to the nations to keep silence before Him. Even if it were now possible to plead their cases, in the executive judgment, He has taken a "just", blameless and irreversible action (cf. Isa 41:1).[175] Now He can say to the Dragon, "The Sovereign Lord will put you to death" (Isa 65:15).

At the beginning of history when the fall of humanity occurred and God pronounced judgment on the serpent, Satan tried to answer back. He tried to make Adam and Eve blame God (cf. Gen

[175] Edward J. Young (1972), The Book of Isaiah, Vol. 3 (Grand Rapids: William B. Eerdmans), 128.

3). And he has tried to use his strategy of blame God for the millennia of history. In the drama of Job, we sense the arrogance of in the opening dialogue. That part of the dialogue only stops when God sent Satan from His presence (Job 1:12, Rev 12:7), and when Job proved Satan false (1:22). At Moses' graveside Satan engaged in a life and death struggle to secure Moses' body. Satan's view was that Moses could not be saved for he had sinned, but God resurrected Moses and took him to heaven, to show the dragon that one is saved by grace not by law keeping (Jude 1:9). In many other times and places God brought Satan to silence (cf. Zech 3:1,2; Matt 4:10; Acts 16:16-18). But it is the final silencing of Satan that is most profound. His pride, his boast, his rebellion against God, his opposition to God, his oppression, his corruption, his deception, his false prophecies, his hatred, his persecution of the saints, his wars, his violence, the idolatry he has sustained, his loud arrogant noises, all will be brought to an end. He and his cohorts will be silenced.

The dragon's punishment is well deserved. First, he will be bound and thrown into 'the bottomless pit" for a millennium (Rev 20:1-3). Then he will be released for a little season to deceive those destined for the second death (Rev 20:7). In the last Great War, he will perform his last great act of deception. He will invite all rebels to the battle of Gog and Magog; the last great battle in the last war. Here the wicked are to be gathered with their leader who will proclaim that he has an opportunity for victory against the people of God (Rev 20:8). But at the same moment, "fire will come down from God out of heaven" to consume the evil host (20:9, 10). Here the dragon will be forever silenced. In the prophecy of Ezekiel that speaks of his end, it is stated that, "By the multitude of your iniquities, in the unrighteousness of your trade, you profaned your sanctuaries, so I brought out fire from within you. It consumed you, and I turned you to ashes on the earth in the sight of all who saw you. All who know you among the peoples are appalled at you; you have come to a dreadful end and shall be no more forever" (Ez 28:18-28). With this destruction of the leader the negative judgment of God is complete. He who sits on the throne will once again be declared Creator and Sovereign. The shout of the universe will be, "You are right in your sentence and blameless in your judgment" (Psa 51:4; Isa 42:26; Rom 3:4; Rev 15:3; 16:7).

God's battle cry has been sounded (cf. Jer 49:2) and the sovereignty of God has been declared. From this perspective one can say that earth and heaven are to be silent. Soon the hosts of heaven will strike up the new worship songs of praise and honor to God, for the judgment of God has been perfected. Let us leave this aside for a future discussion since the one half hour of heavenly silence to which we referenced at the start of our discussion, signals the final fall, destruction, and doom of the self-deifying power. God has investigated all issues. He has vindicated Himself and His people. What more is left is for God bring about his final manifestation. At such a moment the creatures of the universe will turn to worship Him. We shall speak of such worship, but here we conclude with the note of desolation and silence that grips the earth. "The songs of the temple shall become wailings in that day, 'says the Lord God;' the dead bodies shall be many, cast out in every place. Be silent." (Amos 8:3). Edward H. Bickersteth (1875) also says it well:

> Peace, perfect peace, in this dark world of sin
> The blood of Jesus whispers to you
> Peace, peace within.
>
> Peace, perfect peace, our future all unknown?
> Jesus we know, and He is on the throne.

In effect, the dragon's noise has been stopped. Now we can hear what God says, without contradiction.

VII

AFTER THE STORM A CALM: A TIME OF PEACE FOR GOD'S PEOPLE

Be silent; be silent, a whisper is heard;
Be silent, be silent, for holy this place,
Be silent, and listen, Oh, treasure each word.

Tread softly, tread softly, The Master is here;
Tread softly, tread softly, He bids us draw near.
(Fanny J. Crosby, 1820-1915)

After the storm a calm: The return to silence

What has been posited as the action of God against evil is only one half of the story that concerns the judgment that follows from the half an hour of silence in heaven and the sounding of the trumpets (Rev 8ff). In many scriptures it is stated that in the sounding of the trumpet for the judgment of evil, there is also a judgment that brings the complete redemption of the people of God. That is to say, in the destruction of evil is the mercy of God. This aspect of the discussion extends the focus on the tranquility that is to follow the great noise of judgment; after the judgment God will be present with his people without interruption (Rev 19-22). The storms of life may roar and the silence of death may claim everyone, but the One who is in charge of both life and death will destroy even the last enemy (1 Cor 15:26). Thus, having brought the destruction He will bring a new creation (Rev 21:5).

John K. Roth, who has written a powerful response to the late Paul Van Buren on "The Silence of God," in relation to the Holocaust, has said that to transform history into something very different from the "slaughter bench" that Hegel envisioned it to be demands some radical changes. When Roth asks, "Who will carry out the change?" he offers that neither Christians nor Jews are capable of carrying out the change without the grace of God. It is not likely that any human power alone will succeed in turning the world's plowshares and spears into pruning hooks. If lions and lambs are to lie down together in peace on earth, nothing less than a massive intervention from God appears necessary. And if God does not intervene, history will be left less than redeemed. The redemption of history is a theme with which holocaust and other historians need to wrestle.[176] I shall offer in this discussion that only Christ the Messiah can break out of God's eternal silence to transform history.

The redemption of history

The redemption of history is what concludes the judgment of God. Questions that have been raised about God's silence are answered in the judgment and redemption. The redemption has been stated in the historical covenant promises, has been established in the resurrection of Christ, and will be consummated in the final resurrection. In this process of redemption, heaven becomes quiet to hear the cries for the deliverance and justice of God's persecuted servants (Rev 6:10; 8:3). The response to the prayers of the saints is followed by the wrath of God and the departure of the heavenly host from the temple in train with Christ. That is to say, all of the inhabitants of heaven are on their way to take the redeemed back to their heavenly home. As John presents the picture, heaven is the home for the people of God (Rev 21, 22).

---

[176] John K. Roth, "The Silence of God," Faith and Philosophy Vol. 1:4 (October 1984), 407-418.

The half an hour of silence (Rev 8:1) will be a time of challenge for the people of God who are waiting for Christ to take them back to their heavenly home. I need to reflect on the silence from the perspective that John shows in Revelation 19:11-14, where he takes note of the Faithful and True, the Word of God, who is riding on a white horse back to earth with the armies of heaven following. While the saints of God are waiting to sing the great Hallelujahs of redemption, their anxiety, agony and anguish peak as they are opposed, attacked, mocked, and persecuted in the time of waiting for the presence of their Lord and King. For many theologians this is living in the time of Jacob's trouble or the time of the great tribulation.[177]

The last great temptation of the saints

While I was sharing this study of Revelation 8:1 with a friend, he offered that the greatest challenge in the time of silence for the saints will be waiting to see the manifestation of God who has been absent from the temple. I said thanks to him and was able to test his point within a few days when I went to visit my sick brother. I had told my brother that I would come to see him on the weekend, perhaps between Saturday night and early Sunday morning. I called on Wednesday and did not phone again before I reached him. When I reached him on Sunday morning at 10:00 AM, one of our sisters was on the phone with him. When my brother handed the phone to me, my sister told me that she had been speaking to him for a long time. His anxiety had so peaked that he was facing near depression. After I finished speaking with our sister, I completed the greeting with my brother, and then I asked him to describe what had happened. He quickly told me that he had not slept all night. He had been looking out the window all Saturday in the afternoon. Even when he went to the bathroom, he went to a front one because he did not want to miss me if I came.

[177] Cf. William Barclay, (1976, revision), The Revelation of John, Vol 2, (Philadelphia: Westminister Press), 16-17.

The silence, which occurred from Wednesday to Sunday, gave a more profound dynamism to our meeting. So is it not possible that the silence of Revelation 8:1 will enrich the experience of the saints waiting with anticipation for the coming of the King? A common axiom we have used states that "If God is in heaven, then all is well on earth." Even though it does not always seem so, yet Daniel assured king Nebuchadnezzer that "there is a God in heaven" who can tell what is and what is to be (Dan 2:27, 28). Christ said that all authority was given to Him in heaven and on earth (Matt 28:18). Here the question for the saints will be "What happens when God leaves the throne room?" "What happens when God leaves the heavenly temple?" What happens when Christ has left the mercy seat?" One might suspect that this will be a great moment for Satan and his host to unleash their last great temptation against the saints of God. It will be pressed as hard as it was pressed when Christ was in the garden of Gethsemane and hung upon the cross. It will be pressed as when the apostles witnessed the ascension of Christ, and did not find comfort until the Holy Spirit came to take the place of Christ. It will be pressed as when Job's wife came to him and said "Curse God and die," or when the friends of Job gave their false views of the justice of God. At such moments one is torn apart by the challenge of faith. The question will be asked again by the saints, "How long, Oh Lord? How long?"

Waiting for God to speak again

One of the most profound contemporary reflections on the anguish of faith is the novel *Silence* by Shusaku Endo. He bases it upon the history of Christian missionaries in Japan in the mid-sixteenth century. The Christian missionaries who went to Japan then were caught in the midst of a national strife. The Japanese peoples were trying "to find themselves." Therefore any organization, religion or ideology, which seemed to interfere with the national effort to build a harmonious society was taken to be the enemy and was therefore dealt destructive blows. In the midst of the strife and uncertainties, Roman Catholic missionaries from Portugal went to witness for God. Many of the missionaries even made their way into the halls of the revolutionary leadership called the *bakufu*. But they were soon rebuffed, arrested, and often forced into apostasy. Many, including a revered teacher, Father Ferreira, abandoned their faith. On hearing of the apostasy of the famous teacher, one Father Rodriques and his friends went out to find Father Ferreira, to find out why he had given up his faith. Before secretly entering Japan, Father Rodriques secured the services of Kichijoro, a weak and cowardly believer who had denounced his faith on several occasions. Unknown to Rodriques, Kichijoro had received a sum of money from the Japanese authorities for selling the missionaries to them, Rodriques was unaware of this and only heard that Kichijoro had excellent knowledge of the countryside. As could be expected, Kichijoro gave Rodriques the necessary assistance in meeting with some of the Christians who were still in hiding, but also betrayed him to the authorities who promptly arrested him, placed him in prison and brought on the usual pressures to apostatize. The authorities felt that no purpose was served when they martyred the missionaries so they strongly coerced them to apostatize.

When Rodriques was shown the shocking sight of several believers hung upside down in the pit with blood dripping from small holes pierced in their ears, he resolved that he wanted to endure death to save them. He had come to Japan to stop the apostasy, but did not know that the only path that would be opened to him was the way of apostasy. As he listened to the "bark of the guards" and the cries and prayers of the persecuted, and experienced the darkness of the prison cells, and finally the silence of the birds and the cicadas, he had a profound sense that God was silent. He could not perceive why God was not doing something to free the prisoners and punish the guards and the authorities. One day while he was agonizing he was moved to a prison where the authorities had arranged for him to meet Ferreira, whom he had come to seek. In the conversation that followed Rodriques confirmed that Ferreira had apostatized. Now Ferreira was strongly urging Rodriques to apostatize. Among the things Ferreira told Rodriques was, "The reason I apostatized . . . are you ready? Listen! I was put in here and heard the voices of those people for whom God did nothing. God did not do a single thing. I prayed with all my strength but God did nothing." Then he advised Rodriques, "Be quiet! All right. Pray! But those Christians are partaking of a terrible suffering such as you cannot understand. From yesterday – in the future – now at this very moment. Why must they suffer like this? And while this goes on, you do nothing for them. And God – he does nothing either." As these comments brought greater and greater tension upon the heart of Rodriques, he shook his head wildly; putting both fingers into his ears, while the voice of Ferriera and the groaning of the Christians broke mercilessly in. Rodriques cried, "Stop! Stop! It is now that you should break the silence. You must not remain silent. Prove that you are justice, that you are goodness, that you are love. You must say something to prove that you are the august one." At that moment a great shadow passed over Rodriques' soul and he remembered that, as at other times, when he heard the cries of the Christians God was silent. He also remembered that when the misty rain flooded over the sea, God was silent. And when the one-eyed man had been killed beneath the blazing rays of the sun, that God had said nothing. And then he heard more cries of people in the pit. He then turned to God and asked again, "Why is God continually silent while those groaning voices go on?" Ferraira then broke in to point to the fact that he was telling no lie about the silence of God. He argued further that before he had heard the cries he prayed, and kept on praying, but prayer did nothing to alleviate the suffering of those in the pit. "Prayer does nothing to alleviate suffering." After continuing the aggravation to Rodriques' faith, Ferriera finally led Rodriques to think in the radical direction that

Ferriera had taken, namely, that Christ would have rejected God for the sufferers' salvation. The story concludes, when, after much personal misgiving and reflection, Rodriques stamped upon the picture of the face of Jesus (the *fumi),* just as Ferriera had previously done in his apostasy. Rodriques argued that before he stamped upon the *fumi* he could feel the pain in his feet, but then the *fumi* spoke to him and said, "It is alright to step on me. I more than anyone know the pain in your foot. I was born into this world so that people could tread on me. It was to share people's pain that I carried the cross."[178]

By making the latter the best resolution of a faith that confronts the silence of God, Endo seems to fall into the very trap that he might have been seeking to avoid, namely, the belief that in the midst of the silence of God a cul-de-sac confronts the Christian. If this were the case, then, in confronting satanic anger the saints would join the wicked to curse the name of God (Rev 16:8). The incongruities of the divine action might perplex them, but they do not curse God. They will not join the wicked, nor accept any denial of the divine rule. Satan will work to shame them but they will bear it gladly. If Satan offers martyrdom they will also savor it. Like the martyrs of the centuries gone, they will never join Satan and his apostate hosts. As C. Mervyn Maxwell says, when martyrs confront domination they look away from the devil to God.[179] They know that God will choose to listen to them and intervene to aright the injustice against them. Of course, their understanding of the divine judgment does not so much focus on God's penultimate response as on the ultimate response. They trust God for the final judgment.

If we can sense the theology of martyrdom as John gives it to us, we are to thank Endo for his poignant reflection on silence, but suggest that his shortcoming is that he misses a theology of

---

[178] Shusaku Endo (1969), Silence (New York: Taplinger Publishing).
[179] C. Mervyn Maxwell (1985), God Cares: The message of Revelation for You and Your Family, Vol. 2 (Boise, ID: Pacific Press) ,188.

martyrdom.[180] John sees martyrdom as a significant part of Christian life. He reflects upon martyrdom in many chapters of the Apocalypse. Then he reflects upon the comfort that is brought to the martyrs when he shows how God answers. For example, he states that he sees the martyrs drawn from every race, tribe, peoples and tongues, standing before the throne and before the Lamb, with palm branches in their hands, shouting in a great voice that salvation belongs to God, who is seated on the throne forever (Rev 7:9,10). It is a glorious moment as John later says, "And I heard a voice from heaven saying, 'Write this: Blessed are the dead who from now on die in the Lord.' 'Yes,' says the Spirit, 'they will rest from their labors, for their deeds follow them'" (Rev 14:13). John's point is made that though pressures and persecutions will be severe, yet the hearts of the servants of God will be on being in the presence of the King of kings, not on the negative direction of history. They "did not cling to life even in face of death" (Rev 12:11).

A critique made by Chung Ha-Eun concerning Rodriques rightly notes the lack of concern for the faith of his executioners. Chung Ha-eun states that in his prayers Rodriques not only did not pray for his executioners, but he failed to evangelize them. Ha-eun then states that, "A true martyr weeps and prays not only for the believers but also for those who cause the martyrdom. Since there were no such prayers, perhaps this is the reason God did not hear the prayers of the missionaries. There was a reason behind God's silence."[181] When Christ suffered from the cross he prayed a last prayer, "Father, forgive them for they know not what they do." And this is most exemplary for all to do.[182] It must never be thought that all of the servants of God will be martyrs, but each must bear the burden of his/her life with the kind of submission for which Christ calls in every case. Philip Doddridge says that while

---

[180] Chung Ha-Eun, "The Silence of God: A Theological View," The Japan Christian Quarterly (Summer, 1988), 142-149.
[181] Ibid.
[182] Ibid.

we live in the world we may feel a large share of personal or public tribulation; but when it presses hardest upon us, let us lift up our eyes to that glorious scene which the apostle beheld, and which was so excellent and sublime. The scene will well transport us, even under the tribulations through which we must pass to a better hope.[183] He argues, further, that we must persevere steadily and faithfully, as the martyrs of old did; and the day will come, when our robes shall be as white, and our crowns as radiant, and our palms as verdant as theirs. We must try to bear with patience, hunger and thirst, heat and weariness, while we travel through this vale of tears. We must rejoice in hope of the everlasting refreshment and pleasure to which the Lamb will lead us; even those fountains of living water of which He will give us to drink. When God shall wipe away tears from our eyes, and place us before His throne, we shall serve Him day and night in His temple, and see His face, and dwell with Him, and have Him forever. He will dwell with us and in us, without any separation.[184]

In another critique of Endo's work, we might argue that it is of interest to see how an opinioned conception of the Christian faith can drive one to a heretical conclusion. The point that I am noting is the subtle way in which Endo projects idolatry as normative for Christian faith. He notes, for example, that Rodriques suffered because he viewed the *fumi* as a "Holy Image." For a long time Rodriques refused to stamp upon it thinking that it was the living Christ. Even when he stamped he felt he had stamped upon an image that had been transubstantiated. But when idols are thus rationalized they can obscure a person's ability to see reality with transparency or can lead to the tragic silence of which we spoke when we presented the issue of idolatry in an earlier discussion. It is correctly noted that silence can either be the snare of the demon or a sign of an individual's union with divinity. For Kierkegaard often silence takes a person into the negative path of

[183] Philip Doddridge (1833), The Family Expositor (Amherst, MA. J.S. and C. Adams Printers), 919.
[184] Ibid., 919.

self-consciousness so that he/she might even refuse to communicate with others. The greatest tragedy of all is when a person "shuts up" himself/herself in a way that he/she is cut off from the divine revelation.[185] Or let me state this in a different way, that in times of crisis people often abandon their faith (even the truth); thus giving up their hold on God and turning to the dumb idols.

We must therefore constantly take with seriousness the issue that is emphasized in the first of the three great warnings from the angels of Revelation 14:6-12, namely, that the call to worship the true and living God, the Creator of heaven and earth[186] is the primary task of humankind. In noting this call one biblical commentator speaks of Isaiah's record in his forty-first chapter where God addresses the heathen nations, and in particular the inhabitants of the coastlands and islands of the Mediterranean. He notes that while the Lord has already spoken directly to Israel, pointing out the impotence of the idols, He then turns to the worshippers of idols and states in the imperative that the islands are to turn in silence unto Him. God does not intend to participate in a debate as to who is the true and living God. God is above any idol. He does not appear as a party before a judge waiting to hear a verdict pronounced against Him. Rather, He addresses the isles with the voice of His absolute authority. He commands them to turn unto Him in silence. They are to listen to Him and not to the verdict of some "third party," for before his words there can be no answer.[187]

In his radical (if not iconoclastic) critique of idolatry, Jacques Ellul has said that the Church allowed itself to be invaded

---

[185] Ronald Grimsley (1973), Kierkegaard (New York: Charles Scribner's Sons), 66-67. This is a powerful reflection on Kierkegaard's concept of dread in which he observes that silence is an ambiguous thing. And one who is paralyzed by the temporal cannot do otherwise than to choose the demonic side of silence.

[186] Cf. William Barclay (1976, revision), The Revelation of John, Vol 2 (Philadelphia: Westminister Press), 109-110.

[187] Edward J. Young (1972), The Book of Isaiah Vol. 3 (Grand Rapids, MI: Wm. B. Eerdmans), 70, 71.

by images. It did so because it wanted to become visible, that is to establish itself on the foundation of evidence. The idolatry developed along the theology of the Church's power and the lust for power, which became incarnate in the institution. Ellul states that he is terribly sorry that he has to say such unpleasant things about the admirable works produced by Christian artistic flowering, since he understands that the artists themselves were seeking to give praise to God as often they did. In his words it is noted, "I do not at all condemn those who worked with such great perfection as painters, sculptors, and architects. They worked to the best of their ability, with all their faith, consecration, and service, in order to praise and glorify God." He goes on to note that these workers were all simple artisans, and the idolatrous error did not take place on their level. "On the one hand they were marvelous artists, on the other they were dedicated Christians. They wanted to serve God with their art, and, in effect, they did serve him." And, Ellul believes that God surely accepted their work, which is part of the glory of the nations that will be fully integrated in the heavenly Jerusalem. But the error of their work came through the Church that made it seem that their work was eternal. That means that in the Church images became the glorification of humanity and of individuals. The visualizing of God's message brought in its wake all kinds of consequences in terms of magic, superstition, idolatry, paganism, and polytheism. Whether one likes to admit it or not, the abundance of images, ceremonial beauty, the visual triumph of liturgy, and purely visual symbolism were the main sources of the medieval and later errors in the Roman and Orthodox Churches. Art and theology suffered a complete mutation in the centuries of spiritual and human disasters. Thus the word of God today is quite repressed.[188] Max

---

[188]Jacques Ellul (1985), The Humiliation of the Word (Grand Rapids, and MI.: Wm. B. Eerdmans). All of the chapter on "The Religious Conflict Between Image and Word" bears this radical critique of idolatry. It is my conviction that we need to contemplate the issues involved with a sense of seriousness.

Picard says that the exclusive love of pictures and images is a danger to the true nature of humanity. The beauty of pictures and images often only lead people to silence.[189]

One of my strong convictions is that in our image consumer culture, it is quite easy to suffer the mutation of our intelligence and lose the vision of the divine. This is why we need to turn to the Scripture which appeals to us to love the Lord our God with all our heart, and with all our soul, and with all our might (Deut 6:5). For Matthew and Mark this is even extended. "Love the Lord your God with all your heart, and with all your soul, and with all your mind" (Matt 22:37). "Love the Lord your God with all your heart, and with all your soul, and with all your mind, and with all your strength" (Mk 12:30). In effect, the faithful of God who face an idolatrous culture must be deeply discerning, and must resist any call to depend upon an idol to bring about the revelation of truth. A radical critique of our culture will say that the saints cannot worship the beast and "its image" or receive its mark (Rev 14:9). The thoughts of the saints must rest on God and God alone; for it is from Him that they always get their word of command.

A third point of critique is that God is not short on solutions. In the midst of silence God can speak profoundly and protect powerfully. Thus, in the darkest night, in the deepest pit, in the most profound anxiety, agony or anguish, we can expect that somehow God will intervene. The Second Coming of Christ is the answer of God to the prayers of the saints. On the one hand it returns to the earth in wrath – the judgments of God. On the other hand it is salvation for those who have been faithful. The Scripture tells us in many places that "God remembered" His covenant with Noah (cf. Gen. 8:1), Abraham (cf. Gen. 19:29), Isaac, and Jacob (Gen 50:24), and took away the reproach of the house of Israel (Ex 3:16; Psa 98:3). He remembers his covenant with all His faithful ones of the ages. The point is that the people of God are never forsaken or forgotten; though in the midst of their darkest hour, the

---

[189] Max Picard (1952), The World of Silence, (Chicago: H. Regency), 80.

half an hour of silence looks like an eternity, God does not forget. J. A. Seiss says, "Moments of agonizing suspense stretch out in hours and days, in comparison with moments of ordinary life. Two minutes of delay when a man is drowning, is an awful period to have to wait. A stoppage of ten minutes between the words I am speaking, would be an intolerable interval. When on the margin of the realization of great expectations, or interrupted in the midst of what has been absorbing the interests of the soul, every instant of delay expands into hours, and even ages . . ."[190]

Many theological works have been written focusing on the long wait of the saints for the arrival of the Messiah. But they have often noted with assurance that after the awful pause, God once again speaks on behalf of his people. We can speak of the multiple and varied ways in which God intervenes on behalf of His saints, but we shall reserve such for another study. The purpose of this study is to focus on the greatest moment of intervention the world has even known: the opening of the seventh seal. The intervention is what will break the dramatic silence of which we speak. It will answer the question, "How long, Oh Lord?" a question which has been asked by the saints of the ages.

The seventh seal and the Second Coming of Christ

I speak of the seventh seal and the Second Coming, for this is what I noted as one way of interpreting the silence in heaven when the King will ride on the clouds to come with the armies of heaven in His train. This we said would bring our discussion to the high point of all that was to be said. God will leave His throne room to rescue His saints from the hands of evil. The people of God have been judged, it is now time for the judgment of the wicked. And the schema we noted in the ancient prophets is that when the judgment is completed on the nations God will return to restore the heavenly order of worship with His people (cf. Ez 33 ff.

---

[190] J. A. Seiss (1981), The Apocalypse: Lectures on the Book of Revelation (Grand Rapids, MI: Zondervan), 187.

Isa 35 ff.). The picture painted by the prophet Zechariah is that the feet of the Returning One will stand on the Mount of Olives. The Mount of Olives will be split in two from East to West, and half of the mount will withdraw northward and the other half southward to receive the Lord and His host (Zech 14:4). However this is to be understood, it means that the coming of Christ will break the silence of nature. His coming will quake the earth.

The point of ascension (Acts 1:12) is the point of the descent. From this point Christ had looked at the Jerusalem temple and predicted its destruction. From this point He had told of the signs of His coming and the final conflagration. From this point He also told the disciples of the coming of "false Christs" and "false prophets," and the tribulation that they would have to face. He told that because of the testing of faith that some of the faithful would apostatize. He told of the great human transgressions at the end. He said that when the gospel is preached to the entire world the end will come. But He did not tell of the exact time of His coming. This He left in silence. (See Matt 24). But all of the writers of the New Testament tell us that His coming is sure. The author of the Thessalonians says that one of these days:

> The Lord himself, with a cry of command, with the archangel's call and with the sound of God's trumpet, will descend from heaven, and the dead in Christ shall rise first. Then we who are alive, who are left, will be caught up in the clouds together with them to meet the Lord in the air; and so we will be with the Lord forever (1 Thess 4:16,17).

The Royal One will be on His way as the trumpet of triumph is blown (cf. 1 Kings 34:34, 39; 2 Kings 9:13). No vision of a secret rapture is presented to us. In the biblical imagery, the heavens open, the clouds are rolled back, the darkness breaks, and the great manifestation of the King takes place. In effect, Christ descends. Thus the flood of glory that illuminated the sky at Christ's first appearing as a child in a manger is a hundred times more enchanting (Rev 1:7). The great festival is about to be celebrated in the divine temple (cf. Rev 19). The trumpet of praise and the voices of shout in celebration of the victory of God is to be heard. The uncontrollable silence that seemed to have left the saints exposed to a time of intense anxiety and agony is now answered by *the shout*, because God is in the city (Rev 21:22). Whether the saints are standing around the divine throne, in the company of angels, singing praises to the Lamb who sits on the throne, or whether they are sitting at the table in the grand Messianic Banquet Hall, or whether they stand on the divine right hand, God is in the midst of them. God, their **Relentless Lover**, is present with Christ, the divine co-regent, **the Faithful** and **True**, the **Messiah Warrior King**. He is present as Creator, Sustainer, and Ruler. He is present as Lord and King. He through whom the old has passed and the new is to come into being is on the scene. When He speaks out of His silence, the silence that met humanity in the depth of its suffering and pain will be explained. Those who have experienced the silence of death will hear the voice that bids them to take possession of the kingdom.

A time to shout

The saints will join to shout with freedom the phrases that have been their sources of comfort for the millennia of history. One thing they will say is "Death is swallowed up in victory . . . . O Death where is your sting" (cf. 1 Cor 15:54-55). The understanding is that there is nothing to fear, for sin and death has been vanquished. In the history of the world, Satan has always tried to make it seem that he controls the grave. In the times of death, God often seems hidden and elusive. But the resurrection says that God has had the first word and the last word. Those who die in Christ are "changed in a moment, in the twinkling of an eye" (1 Cor 15:51). Transfigured and transformed, they are in their full vigor. The scene of the saints who await the coming of Christ thus changes from anxiety to assurance, from darkness to light, from apprehension to faith, and from death to life. It is a time of peace. It is a time of joy. "There is singing up in heaven such as we have never known." It is a time of rest. To celebrate the new creation, the eternal Sabbath rest begins.

Recreating the earth out of silence

There are commentators who have argued that the "half an hour" of silence represents another creative moment for God. God will recreate the world as he did at first, out of the primeval silence. He will speak a word, as he did at first, and a new day will dawn.[191] We need not make a long discussion of it, but as connected with the Second Coming, John says, "Behold I make all things new" (Rev 21:5). This is how God will confront the silent intruder, the silent invader, and all that hurt and destroy. Every evil things will be destroyed. The continuous state of war and the constant threat of impending danger will be brought to an end.

In a survey of the literature on silence, I have seen a great record of the need for overcoming the silent barriers, the silent cries, the "silent screams," the silent killers, the silent sorrows, the silent griefs, the silent diseases, the silent depressions, "the silence of the children," "the silence of the lambs", the silent suffering, and every other kind of oppressive silence. The same point is made in Scripture: "Then the eyes of the blind shall be opened, and the ears of the deaf shall be unstopped; then the lame shall leap like a deer, and the tongue of the speechless sing for joy" (Isa 35:5-6). Authentic silence is liberative silence, which begins with the great Sabbath of peace. Yes, as the author of Hebrews says, "A Sabbath rest remains for the people of God" (Heb 4: 9).

---

[191] Cf. J. M. P. Sweet (1997), Revelation, (Philadelphia: Westminster Press), 159

The signal of the eternal Sabbath rest

We have noted that the contest among commentators is whether the half an hour of silence could be proleptic of the eternal Sabbath joy or the eternal peace that will exist at the redemption of history. I do not seek to extend the debate, but I find it fascinating to note like the ancient prophets that what follows the time of judgment (even the time of the divine silence) is a period of blessing which is to be followed by the eternal Sabbath (cf. Ez 40-48). At such a time, the glory of God is to return to the temple and the land is to be restored. The pictures painted by the prophets of this millennial time of holiness are fantastic, to say the least. Isaiah states, for example, "For as the new heavens and the new earth which I will make, shall remain before me, says the Lord; so shall your descendants and your name remain. From new moon to new moon, and from Sabbath to Sabbath, all flesh shall worship before me says the Lord" (Isa 66:22-23). In the New Testament, this same Sabbath rest is set forth as the *rest* of God which still remains for the people of God (see Heb 4). The *rest* is a *katapausis* (the heavenly rest or heavenly time of healing) and *sabbathismos* (the eschatological time of jubilee*), which* mean that the saints of God have entered into God's Promised Land. When the author of Hebrews connects the rest of God with the seventh day, he is returning to indicate that the Creator God is the same God who will bring about the newness of life. Whatever else one might interpret from the Old and New Testament authors on the subject, what is clear is that the Sabbath of eternity will be a time of quiet, relaxed, harmonious, joyful, celebration. This grouping of terms might seem a contradiction, but the rest does not contradict the joy. Here it is noted that the convulsions and revolutions that have continued to be a part of the history of time and which are intensified by the Second Coming have come to rest.

The emphasis is that the heavenly sounds will be sane. There will be no competing freeways, airplanes, or other kinds of competitive earthly noises. There will be no need to rush. The relationships between silence and sound will be fully known. The mystical silence for which humans have searched will be manifest – The presence of God will be with humanity. As Guillaume de Saint-Thierry says of the divine silence:

> O Happy, most happy the soul
> that is drawn by grace to God by God,
> so that, through the unity of the Spirit in God,
> it takes no thought of itself,
> …………………………
> This is the end,
> this is the consummation,
> perfection, peace, the joy of God,
> the joy in the Holy Ghost:
> This is Silence in Heaven
>
> Guillaume de Saint-Thierry

The sanctuary of peace is only truly found when God returns to be with humanity. He returns out of silence. He returns from the clouds, which kept Him hidden from view. While He lived on the earth for thirty-three and a half years He was often rejected. And throughout history He has been the rejected, but one of these days He is coming back as King of kings and Lord of lords, to dwell with humanity forever. He returns as the holy *Shekina,* with the hosts of heaven accompanying Him. He will then establish the kingdom of eternal peace. Thus the tree of good and evil will not be present again. The fall and the temptation of humankind will never begin again. Satan will never be able to come near to God's people again. The judgment is stopped. The works of reconciliation and recreation are thus completed. There is then uninterrupted communion with God. This is for me real silence in heaven.

VIII

EMBRACING THE DIVINE SILENCE

God is our refuge and strength,
A well-proven help in troubles.
Therefore we will not fear, though
the earth shall change;
Though the mountains totter in
the midst of the sea;
Though its waters roar and foam;
Though the mountains tremble with its
tumult.
There is a river whose strains make glad
the city of God,
The holy habitation of the Most High.
God is in the midst of the city; it shall
not be moved;
God will help it when the morning
dawns.
The nations are in uproar, the kingdoms
totter;
He utters his voice, the earth melts.
The Lord of hosts is with us,
The God of Jacob is our refuge.
Come; behold the works of the Lord;
What desolations he has made in the
earth.
He makes wars to cease to the end of
the earth;

He breaks the bow, and shatters the spear;
He burns the shields with fire.
Be still, and know that I am God!
I am exalted among the nations,
I am exalted in the earth.
The Lord of hosts is with us;
The God of Jacob is our refuge.
(Psa 46).

Silent Justice

In concluding the reflection on the heavenly silence of Revelation 8:1, it is of interest for me to restate that there is to be a time of silence when all the world will be called to listen to the one who has been the Judge of all the earth. We have also noted how the scriptural prophetic tradition calls the world to listen to the moment of silence (cf. 1 Kings 22:19; 2 Kings 20:16; Isa 1:10; 28:14; Jer 10:1; 19:3; 25:7; Amos 7:16; Matthew 13:15; Rev 3:20, 22; 13:9). For Thomas Merton, the speech of God is silence, but often enough the world resists the silence.[192] The world has been constantly so subjected to speech and noise that it cannot tolerate God's silence. Merton carefully reminds us that what is needed in this world of madness is to lose ourselves completely in God, that we might experience His silence. What is needed, Merton says is perfect silence, supernatural silence.[193] Such silence may not be everywhere, but everyone who has been self-absorbed, refusing to

---

[192] Thomas Merton (1953), The Sign of Jonas (New York: Harcourt, Brace and Co.), 267. In reading the works of Thomas Merton and the Desert Fathers of Europe and Africa who influenced Merton the most, one cannot miss their greatest attention to silence. For Merton, silence was not only an external thing but also an internal action, which is truly attained when every thought, desire and judgment is suspended, leaving us most vulnerable to God. See Merton (1957), The Silent Life (New York: Farrar, Straus), and Thoughts in Solitude (1958), (New York: Farrar, Straus), and other works.
[193] Thomas Merton (1966), Conjectures of a Guilty Bystander (New York: Doubleday), 139.

be vulnerable by humbling himself or herself to hear the voice of God, will some day have to listen to the silence of the judgment. Often enough God uses silence to catch our attention (Job 4-37). But in the culture of noise that encircles the world, the heavenly silence is shut out. And then, as it happened at the death of Christ, so it will happen at the end. The angry tones of the wicked will be will rise to God, but then will face the silence of God. Like the prophet Jeremiah said to Moab, "You also, O Madmen shall be brought to silence" (Jer 48:2; cf. Lk 23:48; 1 Sam 2:9; Psa 91:11,12).[194] Their resentful, resistant, rebellious attitudes will be rebuked (cf. Lk 23:44; 1 Sam 2:10).[195] Their derisive acts will cease (cf. Psa 2:4; Matt 8:12). Their lying lips will be hushed in silence (Psa 9:5; 1 Sam 15:23; 2 Thess 2:3). God will remind them, with thunder and lightning and with other demonstrations, such as happens when one is waving to a crowd of angry people to be still; that they are to be still. God will say: "Be still and know that I am God" (Psa 46:10). Though the wicked will try to speak, their lips will not be able to utter a sound; for a moment, at least, they will be silent with consternation (Zech 2:13; Zeph 1:7). And when God breaks out of His silence, the anxiety of the wicked will turn to panic (Zech 14:13; Jer 49:24). Even without a word from God the wicked will run to the silent rocks and the mountains and beg them to fall on them (cf. Rev 6:12-17). They will fall to the silent earth like dead persons (cf. Matt 25:40; 28:4). They will, as faithful Job said of himself, lay their hands over their mouths (Job 40:4). That means, their Babel is stopped. Their babble ceases. But before their last silence they will acknowledge (in silence and speech) the justice of God.

Satan too, the author of all evil, and his host, will be paralyzed at the manifestation of the divine glory. One is constantly struck when one remembers how Satan argued with God concerning God's justice in regard to Job (Job 1:7-9), or the satanic accusation of Joshua the High Priest while he offered

---

[194] Ellen White (1940 edition), Desire of Ages (Boise, ID: Pacific Press), 751.
[195] Ibid., 756.

sacrifice at the altar (Zech 3:1ff). In either case he mocked and mocked, but was rebuked. One day he will receive his ultimate rebuke (Rev 20:2ff). And though he would wish to avoid it, he too will have to confess the justice of God, before passing into his final silence.

The saints will confront the moment of silence when the justice of God will be manifested in the most superlative way, and, in a way, it will create a certain anxiety for them. But their anxiety will be under-girded by a faith that will challenge any fear and panic (Isa 28:16). According to Lloyd Ogilvie, "Fear has reached epidemic proportions in America. It is contagious." People are becoming infected by it and passing it on to others.[196] One does not need to do an extensive search of contemporary films, books, and other communication media, or interview many persons around the world in order to establish that the hearts of human beings are failing them for fear for the things that they even imagine are coming upon the world. What is challenging is that within our contemporary world many Christians have been crippled by neurotic fear.[197] But my interest is not so much to reflect upon the contemporary epidemic of anxiety, perplexity, panic and despair, which affects the world or Christians today. My interest is to focus on the fact that when Christ puts in His appearance, the people of God will be able to rejoice in the assurance that God has had the last word. William Cowper expressed such assurance this way:

God's purposes will ripen fast
Unfolding every hour.
The bud may have a bitter taste
But sweet will be the flower.
God is his own Interpreter
And He will make it plain.

---

[196] Lloyd Ogilvie (1987), 12 Steps to Living Without Fear (Waco, Texas: Word Books), 15.
[197] Ibid., 15.

The issue that needs to be answered is why the people of God can embrace the heavenly silence at the end.

Justice delayed is not justice denied

When we think of the noises of the present world, we must say thank God for the sounds of silence. The silent sounds have held many secrets, and they are often only understood by the saints, for to them has been given to know the secrets of the kingdom of God (cf. Lk 8:10). But sometimes even the saints cannot unlock the secrets, for they still belong to God (Deut 29:29). God's question to Job needs to be heard often: "Where were you when I laid the foundations of the earth? Tell me if you have understanding" (Job 38:4).

> God does not always tell us things,
> How he is working out his plans
> But in his time and in his way
> He clearly lets us know.
>
> Roy Lessin

I recite that the greatest secrets are in the mystery of the creation and life. Then there is the mystery of death, the mystery of love, the mystery of justice and the mystery of the gospel. All of these are to be made plain at the coming of Christ, which, in many ways today, remains a mystery. "No one knows the day or the hour when the Son of Man is coming" (Mk 13:32). We are only told that it is "near" (Rev 1:3). That we must prepare for it as one prepares for a "thief in the night" (Matt 24:43). While silence has led many humans to struggle between faith and doubt, and while some persons give up on life altogether, such giving up will not be found among the saints. In the midst of silence they hold on to the promises of God. Job says it perfectly: "For I know that my Redeemer lives, and that at the last he will stand upon the earth; and after my skin has been thus destroyed, then in my flesh shall I see God, whom I shall see on my side, and my eyes shall behold, and not another" (Job 19:25-27). The saints understand that while God is concealed in the midst of silence those who trust in Him will be justified. They understand that the greatest manifestation of God arises out of silence.[198] While God is with them nothing terrifies them, in so much, that their faith is destroyed (Psa 46:2-4). They can wait patiently for God and he will hear their cry. He will bring them up out of great and horrible pits and put new songs in their hearts (Psa 40).

Empowered by faith

The point I make here is that implicit faith in Christ will make a difference when the saints face "teeth-gripping" experiences, in so much, that the moment is reduced to silence. I was the only male attending a house prayer meeting when with a note of trepidation, one of the ladies attending asked another after the other prayed, "Are you afraid of the future?" She added, "I was wondering as I listened to your prayer." The woman addressed replied, "No, I am not afraid. I was just thinking of the coming of Christ and trying to compare it with labor pains. Between each pain (that is, when the pain stops) you become more anxious and want to deliver. I just want to see Jesus come."

Actually faith does not stop one's anxiety. It only gives one the motive power to endure hardship, stresses, strains, and persecution, (that, without complaining). The great reality for the children of God at the end is that the season of distress and anguish will require of them a faith that can endure profound weariness. For John, the author of Revelation, there is need for "patient endurance" to obtain salvation (Rev 13:10; 14:12). Philosopher John Hick, who does not seem to express the fervency about the assurance of faith in the Divine Providence that John of the *Apocalypse* offers here, declares that for Christians, all of life is

[198] Thomas Merton (1996), Entering Silence: The Journals of Thomas Merton, Volume 11 edited by Jonathan Montaldo, (New York: Harper Collins).

under the control of a single sovereign will (God) who transcends this present world, and whose fulfillment secures happiness and well being.[199] He goes on to define faith as assurance and states its function as seeing God behind the phenomena of the world. "The catalyst of faith," he says, "is the person of Jesus Christ." Christianity sees God's self-disclosure in Christ taking place in the long process that leads from his presence in the wilderness with ancient Israel to the Second Coming.[200] He notes too that with faith, life's opaqueness fades and the symbols become transparent.[201] I speak of the transparency of silence at the Second Coming of Christ when the greatest mysteries of God will be made plain. There is, for me, the mystery of suffering, the mystery of death, the mystery of human indifference, the mystery of the inertia of the human heart, the mystery of the self-defeating course of humankind, the mystery of the powerful abusing the weak, the mystery of people doing vile things and getting away with them so long, the mystery of divine justice, the mystery of divine love, the mystery of the gospel, and the mystery of eternity. All the silent mysteries have challenged me, as they challenged the prophets, but I have concluded, with the prophets, that the faith by which we approach these silences of the world today (2 Cor 5:7) will find explanation some day (1 Cor 13:12; Mk 10:52).

> When we walk with the Lord in the light of His word,
> What a glory he sheds on our way!
> While we do His good will, He abides with us still,
> And with all who will trust and obey.
>
> Not a shadow can rise, not a cloud in the skies,
> But His smile quickly drives it away;

---

[199] John Hick (1957), Faith and Knowledge (Ithaca, New York: Cornell University Press), 215.
[200] Ibid., 215.
[201] Ibid., 215.

Not a doubt nor a fear, not a sigh nor a tear,
Can abide while we trust and obey.

Trust and obey, for there's no other way
To be happy in Jesus, but to trust and obey.
J. H. Samuels (1864-1919).

To the saints, at the end, silence brings healing and wholeness. Silence will draw their lives together. Silence will bring them to the fullest point of their existence.[202]

Satisfied with God's justice

A point I have emphasized when I argued that the saints are able to endure the heavenly silence in the end is the justice of God. The saints have participated in the greatest challenge in the earthly historical pilgrimage for sinners and saints alike. That is, they have wrestled with the question of the divine justice. They want to know "Why? Why Lord? Why the hunger? Why the oppression and violence?" "Why the wars?" "Why all of the satanic destruction?" Why have the seats of satanic power seemed to be in control so long? Why do innocent children have to be abused? In human history a great disjunction has sometimes been created between the justice and the mercy of God – between the law and the love of God. Those who create the disjunction never practice true justice or live according to the principles of love. Only the saints who know that the justice of God accords with the will, that in the character of God there is unity and holy action, only the saints can feel the satisfaction of trusting the divine justice. The saints have known that the justice of God is mixed with mercy and are thankful for it. They have known that where God is judge there is justice and they appreciate it.[203]

---

[202] Thomas Merton (1958), Thoughts in Solitude (New York: Farrar, Straus).
[203] Carl F. H. Henry (1999 edition), God, Revelation and Authority Vol. VI: God Who Stands and Stays (Waco, TX: Word Books), 402-417.

I have preached a sermon titled “Rascals for Judges,” when reflecting on the trial of Jesus before Annas, Caiphas, the Sanhedrin, Herod, Pilate, and the Roman court; and I concluded that it is tragic that too many courts on the earth reflect the character of those courts. While not all courts of the earth are intentionally unjust, the possibilities exist for injustice in every human court. Human injustice, the strong over the weak, the abuse of power seems to be the best description of every court on the earth, for at one time or another judges misread the power play in which they themselves become involved. But in the cosmic court where God pronounces sentence, justice is absolutely justice, and humanity can be satisfied to pronounce that God is just. From the angel(s) (Rev 16:5), and the altar (Rev 19:2), and all that witness the advent of Christ, there will be the shout: “Just and true are your ways, King of the nations.” “You are true and faithful, Lord, for you have judged justly.” While Satan and the wicked have proven the justice of God as a fact and they must acknowledge it, the righteous experience the justice of God and praise God for it. In a word, the righteous have not lived by “hear-say” but have lived within the personal presence of the Judge with whom they have communicated. Now they understand that justice delayed is not justice denied.

Sustained by grace

Satisfaction with the divine justice is connected to the understanding of the divine grace (or mercy), for grace is the other side of the divine justice. There is a loving Father, a resurrected Christ, and a Spirit of power behind the word *grace*. Although John’s only references to grace in Revelation are in his greeting at the beginning (Rev 1:4), and in the salutation in his conclusion (Rev 22:21), yet grace forms a powerful theme in His apocalyptic perspective. Around the throne all of the saved of God will be gathered, being attended by the Shepherd of the host (cf. Rev 7). Apart from this grace, John could not present Christ as a priest

(Rev 4, 5), or as a shepherd of His sheep (Rev 7), or offer the possibility for victory of the saints in the time of trial. The grace of God fortified the martyrs to endure noisy abuses, blows, stoning, dragging along the ground, imprisonment, crucifixion, being thrown to beasts in the amphitheaters, and every other kind of evil heaped upon them. As an indication of their access to the throne of grace, the saints sing even today: "Great and amazing are your deeds, you King of the ages" (Rev 15:3). Or as a modern songwriter puts it:

> Marvelous infinite matchless grace,
> Freely bestowed on all that believe!
> You that are longing to see His face,
> Will you this moment His grace receive?
>
> Julia Johnson (1911).

Encircled by love

Nothing is so reassuring as the divine love. To know that God loves us, even when He rebukes and reproves us (Rev 3:19) that is, even when He brings judgment against us, or is testing us in silence, is a very encouraging thought. Here I do not seek to write a long treatise on love but to simply note how we can understand the love of the divine in the hour of silence as we contemplate a human frame such as couples strolling silently, hand-in-hand, in a park. Here they show a depth of relationship that no words can describe. There is nothing pretentious here. There is silence. But the silence does not diminish the love that enriches it. One who understands the love of God knows that the providence of God works through silence. Thus one may not see the beginning or the central point of the distance flown but can always be thankful, at the end, for the way in which the Lord has piloted.

A repeated fact we have stated in the discussions is that, when the struggle between good and evil, righteousness and wickedness is over, God will make known the silent past. We state at the point of conclusion again "In silence there is God." We can reflect on the storm on the Sea of Galilee and remind ourselves of the voice of Jesus commanding, "Peace be still." The angry waves became still. So in the end, Christ will command the convulsing earth "Be still," and there will be peace and quiet. Many biblical authors have spoken with the conviction that Christ has the keys of death. He can command every silent dead to come forth from the grave. This understanding of the Divine power has helped the saints of the ages to see that God is not controlled by outward circumstances. They see that when things get desperate God is not frightened. They can fix their eyes on the throne from which their King and Shepherd is taking care of them. They know that He is the friend forever. He is the portion of His people. He is the eternal delight.

Drawn by eschatological hope

In addition to faith, grace and love, nothing can so keep an individual through a moment of silence as hope. It is even more fundamental when we think of the eschatological hope. That is the reality that even though the silence of darkness encircle us, we can appeal to the future and assert faith in the ultimate vindication of God (Job 19:23-27). While John does not so much as use the word "hope" in the *Apocalypse*, hope is its theme. He speaks of Christ as "the Coming One" (Rev 1:7; 3:10, 11; 22:7), thus articulating the final hope. Paul makes the point in Titus that the saints await the "blessed hope" (Titus 2:13), that is the hope at the Omega Point. Peter says that through His mercy God has given to us a "living hope" (1 Pet 1:3). I often say such speech joins in the anticipation that has formed the central truth of all of the prophetic Scriptures. Thus when John says in his Gospel, "Do not let your hearts be troubled. Believe in God, believe also in me. In my Father's house are many dwelling places. If it were not so, would I have told you that I go to prepare a place for you? And if I go and prepare a place for you, I will come again and take you to myself, so that where I am, there you may be also" (Jn 14:1-3), he uses a formula that catches the heartbeat of every saint who has suffered the challenges of the hopeless world. The words of an unknown poet to which S. Hibbard (1869) puts music, throb with the same inspiration:

How cheering is the Christian's hope,
While toiling here below!
It buoys us up while passing thro'
this wilderness of woe.

It points us to a land of rest,
Where saints with Christ will rest;
When we shall meet the loved of earth,
And never part again.

For contemporary theologian Jurgen Moltmann and his heirs, hope is the greatest authentication of the Christian Church and of God. Christian hope is more than a simple future anticipation (*futurum*), it is a hope grounded in the advent (*adventus and parousia*) of Christ. I do not care to expand upon the philosophical discussion here, except to state with one of my past professors, Christopher Morse, who was one of Moltmann's students, that "God the Promisor, promises to be present" with us.[204] The one who often seems inaccessible is the Blessed Hope (Titus 2:13). Those of us who patiently endure will obtain the promise of the presence of Christ (cf. Jn 3:14-16; Heb 6; 10; 11). We will know then that we were not being given the silent

---

[204] Christopher Morse (1979), The Logic of Promise in Moltmann's Theology (Philadelphia: Fortress Press), 125. Morse reviews and expands Moltmann's perspective on hope by noting the significance of speech in understanding hope. The issue is that there is a difference in the way the Greeks spoke about hope and the way the Christian speaks. While for the Greeks hope is temporal and logical, as ideas are temporal and sometimes logical, for Christians hope is ontological, eternal and revelatory and is directed from the cross to the Second Advent of Christ.

treatment forever, for God never ceases to protect the faithful, though sometimes He seems to give the silent treatment to catch our attention.

Excited by the presence of God

This is the issue to which we have been projecting; namely that even in the midst of silence God is present. He is present as Lover. He is present as the Just Judge. He is present as a Providential Protector, and one day He will break through the mystery of his silence to be manifest forever. "Then the Lord answered Job out of the whirlwind:" (Job 38:1; 40:1). The point here is that there will be no more interrupted communion. God will not be walking in the garden in the cool of the day, asking "Adam, where are you?" "Eve where have you been?" He will not be breaking through a whirlwind asking Job, "Where were you when." No one will go into the abyss or into solitary places to find God or to hear the voice of God. The God of the wilderness will be seen without disruption. He will be seen and heard everywhere. Yes, "the home of God is among mortals, He will dwell with them as their God; and they will be his people; and God himself will be with them and be their God" (Rev 21:3). There will not be need for anyone to go to a temple to find God – the temple will be everywhere. The saints will live forever in his presence. Their anxiety will turn into perfect joy. And like Job they will answer the Lord, "I know that you can do all things, and that no purpose of yours can be thwarted" (Job 42:2).

Shattering the heavenly silence

In his concluding Upper Room discourse with his disciples, Jesus confronted the anxiety of his disciples thus: "But because I have said these things sorrow has filled your hearts" (Jn 16:6). "You have pain now; but I will see you again, and your hearts will rejoice, and no one will take away your joy from you" (Jn 16:22).

This is all we need to say, that the life-sickening situations of tears and mourning that confront the human race, and especially the people of God, while the wicked rejoice and perpetuate their acts of evil against the innocent, will cease. As Martin Runel says, "*Out of Silence: [There will be] A Journey into Language.*"[205] God will speak again as he spoke at first. The people of God will speak, as they have wanted to speak. The wicked will say with James Calvin Schapp, "*In the Silence there are Ghosts.*"[206] This means that they have come to their dead end with their inarticulate sounds of panic. But the saints of God will sing, as with Anna Waring (1820-1910) and Felix Bartholdy Mendelssohn (1809-1847):

In heavenly love abiding,
No change my heart shall fear;
And safe is such confiding,
For nothing changes here.
The storm may roar without me,
My heart may low be laid,
But God is round about me,
And can I be dismayed?
But God is round about me,
And can I be dismayed?[207]

The mystery of the silence has been broken, just as when one goes to hear an orchestra and waits for the last moment before the music. As the conductor comes out and flips the baton, the music starts. Lawrence Cunningham says, "The silence heightens the passion of the orchestra, the promise of the music, and the

---

[205] Martin Runel (1994), Out of Silence: A Journey into Language (New York: H. Holt). In this work Runel makes the point that language always arise out of silence.

[206] James Calvin Schapp (1995), In the Silence there are Ghosts (Grand Rapids, MI: Baker Books).

[207] Church Hymnal, of the Seventh-day Adventist Church (1941), (Takoma Park, Washington, D, C. Review and Herald).

expectancy of the audience." The music then breaks in and then fades from a finite stretch of time, bounded on both sides by silence (how we hate premature applause at a concert's end!). Without that silence, the music would be a garble. The silence, paradoxically, is heard along with music. The silence is not only necessary for the beginning and end of the music; silence renders the music intelligible in its very performance. Without moments of rest, pause, and stop, there would be no music.[208] The heavenly time that follows the breaking of the silence of which John speaks, is eternity. Paul rightly shows us that we are caught up in language about which we might as well be silent, for, "What no eye has seen, nor ear heard, nor the human heart conceived, [is] what God has prepared for those who love him." (1 Cor 2:9).

The prophetic note of the Bible is clear that when God proclaims the "*finis*" in His work of judgment and salvation, Jesus will come to take His loved ones to their heavenly home. Jacques Ellul calls heaven "a new creation of reality," in which there is no possibility for suffering and death to triumph. The new creation comes together in new-found unity of reality and truth, as the glory of creation answers the Creator's glory in perfect harmony.[209] Here faith will turn to sight. The veil will be removed from our eyes. The ear of the deaf will be unstopped. The tongue of the dumb will sing. Death will be swallowed up in victory. The reproach of God's people will be taken away (cf. Isa 25:3-8). Idols will pass away. The seats of human power – Babylon, Rome, Egypt, Washington, Moscow, London, Damascus and Jerusalem – will be destroyed, and God will set up a kingdom that will last forever (Dan 2:44-45). There is to be then no contradiction between the heavenly silence and the songs of heavenly praise. After the long silence of waiting on God to speak, in the time between the promise and the appearing, the moment comes when

---

[208] Lawrence Cunningham, "On the Silence of God: Some Reflections," Epiphany. 3:1 (Fall 1982): 64-67.

[209] Jacques Ellul (1970), The Meaning of the City (Grand Rapids, MI.: Wm. B. Eerdmans), 172.

the saints will hear the voice of God at the gate to the throne room of divine rule: "Come, My people, enter your chambers, and shut your doors behind you; hide yourselves for a little while until the indignation is past" (Isa 10:25, 26:20). And the reality that God has been involved in their situation leads the saints to break out in worship songs such as they have never sung.

I reflect often on the words of James Weldon Johnson's poem "Lift Every Voice and Sing," written to celebrate the one-hundredth anniversary of Abraham Lincoln's birth. Being very aware that the last lines of the third verse speak to the fact of a national spirit, I note the transcending message which focuses on the final victory of those who seek their liberation from the forces of oppression that have held them captive for many millennia. Often in their condition of oppression they have been subjected to living in bitterness and hatred, destroyed freedom, and deceptive silence. But when God works out His justice, then they get the opportunity to end the falsehood of their silence. The words of the song follow:

> Lift every voice and sing, 'til earth and heaven ring,
> Ring with the harmonies of liberty:
> Let our rejoicing rise, high as the list'ning skies,
> Let it resound loud as the rolling sea.
> Sing a song full of the faith that the dark past has
> taught us,
> Sing a song full of the hope that the present has
> brought us,
> Facing the rising sun of our new day begun,
> Let us march on 'til victory is won.
>
> Stony the road we trod, bitter the chast'ning rod,
> Felt in the days when hope unborn had died;
> Yet with a steady beat, have not our weary feet
> Come to the place for which our fathers sighed?
> We have come over a way that with tears has been

watered.
We have come treading our path through the blood of the slaughtered,
Out from the gloomy past, 'til now we stand at last
Where the white gleam of our star is cast.

God of our weary years, God of our silent tears,
Thou who has brought us thus far along the way;
Thou who has by thy might led us into the light,
Keep us forever in the path, we pray.
Lest our feet stray from the places our God
Where we met Thee, lest our hearts drunk with
The wine of the world, we forget. . . Thee
Shadowed beneath Thy hand may we forever stand,
True to our God, true to our native land.

The manifestation of love that comes after the long night of silence truly calls for a response. This may be as it is above or it may be some "new song" (Rev 14:3), or the song of Moses and the Lamb, with its chorus, "Great and amazing are your deeds, Lord God the Almighty! Just and true are your ways, King of the nations!" (Rev 15:3). Or it might be the Hallelujah Chorus with the great crescendo (Rev 19). However it is or will be, it will be a time when the heavenly silence is broken. God who seemed not to have spoken within certain moments of our lives will explain many things most transparently. God will tell us then why this and why that. He will bring words to our sorrow, and songs to our night of pain. He will speak so that his people who have waited in silence to speak can speak again. In one of his reflections Thomas Merton recites the poetic words of a woman to whom he had listened. In reporting a truck accident she had just observed, the woman said of the driver:

He tried to whistle and he couldn't whistle.
He tried to talk and he couldn't talk.

> He couldn't do nothing and he looked like a nigger with all that cement over him.[210]

Forget any ugly word in the middle of the last sentence. My reason for using what in some view might be the out-of-date words of a woman who was only describing an accident, is to emphasize that many persons have been trapped in an oppressive silence, and that only by the manifestation of grace will they be able to break the silence. Many have tried to speak, whistle, pray, cry, or sing, but have not been able to in the long history of time. Ralph Wiley's book *Why Black People Tend to Shout: Cold Facts and Wry Views From a Black Man's World* might seem apologetic and frivolous from many persons' perspective, but one might say he makes profound sense when he takes note of the fact that Black people were oppressed in slavery with bits in their mouths to stop them from speaking while working, and masks over their mouths to stop them from eating the sugar cane while they were in the canebrake, and treated like aliens to the planet for all of their lives because of their skin color. Then when they sense joy and happiness and freedom, even for brief moments of life, they shout and laugh. I am still to do my research on why Blacks and Jews are so steeped into music, but I have a prejudiced hunch that there is something about subjecting a person to silence for a long time that makes them write Psalms, Oratorios, Spirituals, Blues and Gospel songs. It is a curious fact that often those from outside these traditions and many from inside these traditions who have known little of the experiences of suffering from the previous generations, can trivialize the music. In heavenly history there will be none to forget. When God breaks the code of silence all saints and martyrs who have been oppressed and made silent will join the heavenly choir to sing the grand hallel. God will give them a voice to express themselves. God will give them a new song to sing.

---

[210] Thomas Merton (1966), Conjectures of a Guilty Bystander (New York: Doubleday), 140.

Not just a song in dissonant tones, but a song with heavenly tones. After the interlude of silence, there will be sounds again.

What has been said throughout is simply this, that whether the heavenly silence is a silence of the divine voice that interrupts the ongoing conversation in the dialogue of revelation, or whether it is the turning of God's back on the arrogance of humanity in judgment, the silence that confronts humanity at the end is awesome. Whether it is the silence of the heavenly hosts who participate in the story of salvation, or whether it is the silence in which the saints participate when they confront the most oppressive moments of their lives, the silence is poignant. But one of these days all depressing silences will be broken. Thus, if the story of the second coming of Christ begins with an interlude of silence that breaks into the heavenly sounds, it will conclude with the trumpet of God and the voice of the Archangel, and the shout of the saints who will join with the hosts in the greatest of hallelujah praise.

Yahweh is greater than all gods. He speaks and lets His people speak. He shows forth His power and lets His people praise. The praise of Christian worship has been about the power and the grace of God. And at the end the praise will be perfect. Since many references have been made to the hallelujahs in the *Apocalypse* already, let us take note of a great reference of praise from one of the apocalyptic passages in Jeremiah, namely: "The voice of mirth and the voice of gladness, the voice of the bridegroom and the voice of the bride, the voices of those who sing, as they bring thank offering to the house of the Lord: 'Give thanks to the Lord of hosts, for the Lord is good, for his steadfast love endures forever!'" (Jer 33:11,12). Add to this the praises of the Psalms that are not to be quoted here. But from the latter it is to be noted that after the words of lament concerning the silence (or evident absence) of God, and the prayers of intercession for the help of God, then comes the praises, extolling the might acts of God's salvation. Throughout the Psalms there is praise of God, for His unfailing love in silencing the enemies of Israel (Psalm

143:1,12). The praises include new songs and the full orchestra (Psa 150). As it is noted in the Psalms, so in Revelation there is point of emphasis that the victory of God and His people call for ***pure worship celebration.*** God is the just and compassionate judge God is Sovereign and Creator. He is Lord and Savior. He has silenced the enemy and given a voice to His people (Rev 19).

INDEX

BIBLIOGRAPHY

"A Last Stop Before Heaven." Newsweek (April 7, 1997): 32.

Abery, Gil. "The Silence of God: A Reminiscence about Isaac Bashevis Singer," Tikkuen 9:3 (Jan-Feb, 1994): 61-63.

Abrams, M. H. 1988, "Apocalypse: Theme and Romantic Variations," in TheRevelation of St. John the Divine. Edited by Harold Bloom. New York: Chelsea House.

Allard, Paul. 1907, Ten Lectures on the Martyrs. San Francisco: Harper.

Balthasar, Hans Urs Von. Translated by John Dury. 1971, The Theology of Karl Barth. New York: Harper and Brothers.

Barclay, William. 1960, The Revelation of John, Vol. 2. Philadelphia: Westminster Press.

______ 1976, The Letter to the Hebrews: The Daily Study Bible. Philadelphia: Westminster Press.

Barnes, Albert. 1858, Notes, Explanatory and Practical on the Book of Revelation. New York: Perennial Library.

Barnhouse, Donald Grey. 1971, Revelation, an Expository Commentary. Grand Rapids, Michigan: Zondervan.

Barth, Karl. 1956, Church Dogmatics IV:I The Doctrine of Reconciliation. Edinburgh: T & T Clark.

Barth, Karl. 1989 impression, Church Dogmatics: IV: 2: The Doctrine of Reconcilation. Edinburgh: T & T Clark.

Barth, Markus. 1971, Justification. Grand Rapids, MI: Wm. B. Eerdmans.

Boers, Arthur P. 1991, On Earth as in Heaven: Justice Rooted in Spirituality. Scottday, PA: Herald Press.

Braque, Remi. "The Importance of the Word: The God Who Said it All," Diogenes 54 (Summer 1995): 142-149.

Bromiley, Geoffrey. Editor. 1988, The International Standard Bible Encyclopedia, Vol. 4. Grand Rapids, MI: Wm. B. Eerdmans.

Brown, Raymond E. et al, Editors, 1968, Jerome Biblical Commentary. Englewood Cliffs, NJ: Prentice-Hall, Inc.

Boff, Leonardo. 1978 translation, Jesus Christ Liberator. New York: Obris.

Brunner, Emil. 1943, The Divine-Human Encounter. Philadelphia: Westminster Press.

Buber, Martin. 1957, The Eclipse of God. New York: Harper Touch Books.

Calvin, John. 1950 edition, Institute of the Christian Religion. Vol. 1 edited by JohnMcNeil. York: Holt, Rinehart & Winston.

Chambers, Oswald. 1935, My Utmost for His Highest. Uhrichsville, OH.: Barbour & Co.Inc.

Charles, R.H. 1920, A Critical and Exegetical Commentary on the Revelation of St. John. ICC. Edinburgh: T & T Clark.

Chevalier, Jacques. 1930, Pascal. New York: Longman's, Green & Co.

Cunningham, Lawrence. "On the Silence of God: Some Reflections." Epiphany. 3:1 (Fall 1982): 64-67.

Dausenhauer, Bernard P. 1980, Silence: The Phenomenon and Its Ontological Significance. Bloomington, Ind: Indiana University Press.

Davis, R. Dean. 1992, The Heavenly Courtroom Judgment of Revelation 4-5. Latham, MD: University Press of America.

Diederiu, Donald. 1963, The Right of an Accused in a Criminal Trial not to Refuse to Testify Against Himself According to the Norm. Rome: Officium Libri Catholic, Catholic Book Agency.

Doddridge, Philip. 1833 edition, The Family Expositor. Amherst, MA: J.S. & C. Adams.

Edersheim, Alfred. 1919, The Temple: Its Ministry and Services: As They Were at the Time. London: Religious Tract Society.

Eller, Vernard. 1974, The Most Revealing Book of the Bible. Grand Rapids, MI: Wm. B. Eerdmans.

Elliot, E. B. 1862, A Commentary on the Apocalypse. Vol. 1. London: John Childs & Sons.

Ellul, Jacques 1985, The Humilation of the Word. Grand Rapids, MI: Wm. B. Eerdmans.

______ 1970, The Meaning of the City.Grand Rapids, MI: Wm. B. Eerdmans.

Elshtain, Jean Bethke. "The Hard Questions: Why Heaven Can Wait." The New Republic. (May 5, 1997): 23.

Endo, Shusaku. 1969, Silence. New York: Taplinger Publishing Co.

Flew, Anthony and MacIntyre, Alisdair, editors. 1955, New Essays in Philosophical Theology. New York: Macmillan.

Finger, Thomas. 1991, Christian Theology: An Eschatological Approach. Vol. I. Kitchener, Ontario: Herald Press.

Ford, J. Massyngberde, editor 1975, The Anchor Bible: Revelation. Garden City, NY: Doubleday & Co.

Fowl, Stephen E. 1997, The Theological Interpretation of Scripture. Cambidge MA: Blackwell.

Gaebelein, Frank, E. general editor. 1986, The Expositor's Bible Commentary, Volume 6 (Isaiah-Ezekiel). Grand Rapids, MI: Zondervan.

________ 1981, The Expositor's Bible Commentary, Vol. 12. Grand Rapids, MI: Zondervan.

Gardner, Edmund Garratt. 1970, Dante's Ten Heavens: A Study of the *Paradiso*. New York: Haskel House.

Gardiner, Eileen. Editor, 1989, Visions of Heaven and Hell Before Dante. New York: Italica Press.

Gowan, Donald E. 1994, Theology in Exodus: Biblical Theology In Form of a Commentary. Louisville, Ken.: Westminster John Knox Press.

Grimley, Roland. 1973, Kierkegaard. New York: Charles Scribner's Sons.

Grossberger, Lewis. "Paradise Found." Mediaweek. Vol. 7 (March 24,1997): 48.

Guenther, Margret. "Embracing the Silence." Christian Century. 12:19 (June 7-14, 1995): 603.

Gulley, Noman. 1998, Christ is Coming. Hagerstown, MD: Review and Herald.

Ha-Eun, Chung. "The Silence of God: A Theological View." The Japan Christian Quarterly. (Summer, 1988): 142-149.

Haines, Dorothy."Vacancies in Heaven: the Doctrine of Replacement and Genesis" Notes and Queries. 44 (June 1997) 150-154.

Hall, T. Edward. 1959, The Silent Language. Garden City: Doubleday.

Hamilton , John A. T. 1963, Honest to God. Philadelphia: Westminster Press.

Harris, Thomas Lake. 1894, Conversation in Heaven: a Wisdom Song. Santa Rosa, CA: Fountaingrove.

Hassan, Ihab Habib 1925, 1968, The Literature of Silence: Henry Muller & Samuel Beckett. New York: Knopf.

Hayford, Jack. (Posted on Internet: June 24, 1997). "Silence and Sensitivity," Ministries Today, 3.

Hedges, Stephen J. "WWWMasssuicide.com." US News and World Report, (1997, April 7): 26-30.

Hedges, Stephen. "How an Obscure Cult Mixed Computers, UFOs, and New Age Theology so Its 39 Members Could Take the Ultimate Journey." U.S. News and World Report (April 7, 1997): 25-28.

Henry, Carl F. H. 1983, God, Revelation and Authority, Vol VI: God Who Stands and Stays. Waco, Texas: Word Books.

Henry, Matthew. 1961 edition, Concise Commentary on the Whole Bible. Grand Rapids, MI: Zondervan.

Heschel, Abraham J. 1955, God in Search of Man: A Philosophy of Judaism. New York: Farrar, Straus and Giroux.

Heschel, Abraham.1962, The Prophets. New York: Harper & Row.

Hick, John. 1957, Faith and Knowledge. Ithaca, New York: Cornell University Press.

Hobe, Phyllis. 1987, The Wonder of Prayer. Carmel, New York: Guidepost.

Hopper, Jeffery. 1987, Understanding II: Reinterpreting Christian Faith for Changing Worlds. Philadelphia: Fortress Press.

Hunt, Dave. 1988, Whatever Happened to Heaven? Eugene, OR: Harvest House.

Hutchens, Benjamin. "Religious Silence and the Subversion of Dialogue: The Religious Writings of Edmond Jabes." Literature and Theology, 9: 4, (December 1995,): 423-429.

Ingersol, Robert. 1990 edition, On the Gods and Other Essays. Buffalo, NY: Prometheus Books.

Jaroslav, Jan Pelikan. 1959, Luther the Expositor: Introduction to the Reformers Exegetical Writings. Saint Louis, MO: Concordia Publishing House.

Jung, Carl. 1954, Answer to Job: The Problem of Evil: Its Psychological and Religious Origins, Cleveland Ohio: The World Publishing Company.

Kanipe, Jeff "The Relativity of Heaven." Astronomy, 24 (1996, Feb): 20-21.

Kierkegaard, Soren. 1983, Fear and Trembling, Repetition. Translated by Howard Hong and Edna Hong, Princeton, New Jersey: Princeton University Press.

King, Robert G. 1979, Fundamentals of Human Communication. New York: Macmillan Publishing Co.

Knohl, Israel. "Between Voice and Silence: The Relationship Between Prayer and Temple Cult," Journal of Biblical Literature. 115 (1996): 1

Kraus, C. Norman. 1993, The Community of the Spirit. Waterloo, Ontario: Herald Press.

_______ 1991, God Our Savior: Theology in a Christological Mode. Scotsdale, Penn.: Herald Press.

Kung, Hans. 1978, On Being a Christian Translated by Edward Quinn. New York: Doubleday.

Ladd, George Eldon. 1972, A Commentary on the Revelation of John. Grand Rapids, MI: Wm. B. Eerdmans.

Larkin, Clarence. 1919, The Book of Revelation. Third Edition. Philadelphia: Moyer & Lotter.

Larson, Ralph. 1998, The Hellish Torch. United States. Self Published.

Layman, Charles M. editor, 1971, The Interpreter's One Volume Commentary on the Bible. Nashville, TN and New York: Abingdon Press.

LeBlanc, Jill. "The Act of Silence," Philosophy Today, (1995, Fall): 325-328.

Lenski, R.C.H. 1957, The Interpretation of St. John's Revelation. Columbus, OH: Watburg Press.

Linnemann, Eta. 1990, Historical Criticism of the Bible: Methodology or Ideology: Reflections of a Bultmannian Turned Evangelical. Translated by Robert W. Yarbrough. Grand Rapids, MI.: Baker Book House.

Lloyd, Samuel T. "The Silence of Prayer." Sewanee Theological Review. 35:2 (1992): 158-172. Markquart, Edward. 1985, Quest For Better Preaching: Resources for Renewal in the Pulpit. MN: Augsburg.

Matheson, Tom. "Hamlet's Last Word." Shakespeare Survey, 48 (1995): 113-121.

Maxwell, C. Mervyn. 1985, God Cares: The Message of Revelation for You and Your Family. Vol. 2. Boise, ID: Pacific Press.

McCumsey, Elizabeth. 1987. "Silence." The Encyclopedia of Religion. Vol. 13. General editor Mircea Eliade. 321-324.

McDannell, Colleen. 1990, Heaven: A History. New Haven, CT: Yale University Press.

Melchert, Charles F. "Learning from Suffering, Silence, and Death." Religious Education 84 (1989, Winter): 34-47.

Merton, Thomas. 1966, Conjectures of a Guilty Bystander. Garden City, NY: Doubleday.

______1995, Entering the Silence: Becoming a Monk & Writer. San Francisco: Harper.

______ 1996, Entering Silence: The Journals of Thomas Merton. Volume Two. Edited by Jonathan Montaldo. New York: Harper Collins.

Merton, Thomas (1997). Learning to Love: Exploring Solitude and Freedom. San Francisco: Harper.

______1953, The Sign of Jonas. New York: County Life Press.

______1958, Thoughts in Solitude. New York: Farrar, Straus.

Minear, Paul et al, editors. 1998, New Testament Apocalyptic. Nashville, TN: Abingdon Press.

Morris, Leon. 1987, Revelation: Tyndale New Testament Commentaries. Grand Rapids, MI: Wm. B. Eerdmans.

Morse, Christopher.1979, The Logic of Promise in the Moltmann's Theology. Philadelphia: Fortress Press.

Neher, Andre. 1981, The Exile of the Word: From the Silence of the Bible to the Silence of Auschwitz. Philadelphia: The Jewish Publications Society of America.

Nesti, Arnaldo. "Silence as Elsewhere," Social Compass. 42:4 (1995): 421-431.

Nichol, F. D. general editor. 1980 printing, Revelation: The Seventh-day Adventist Bible Commentary, Volume 10. Washington, DC: Review and Herald.

Niebuhr, Reinhold.1974, Justice and Mercy. Edited by Ursula M. Niebuhr. New York: Harper and Row.

O'Donovan, Leo J. and Sanks, Howland T. Editors. 1989, Faithful Witness: Foundations of Theology for Today's Church. New York: Crossroads.

Ogilvie, Lloyd.1987, 12 Steps to Living Without Fear. Waco, Texas: Word Books.

Ono, Yoko. "Levelheads Lyrics . . . Calm Before the Storm" http://www.kcs.com.au/~boomdocks/lyrics/valm4.htm.

Pannenberg, Wolfhart. 1968, Revelation as History. New York: Macmillan.

Paulien, Jon. 1992. "The Seven Seals," In Symposium on Revelation Book I. Edited by Frank Holbrook. Silver Spring, MD: Biblical Research Institute.

Phillips, John. 1987. Exploring Revelation, Chicago: Moody Press.

Picard, Max. 1952. The World of Silence. Chicago: H. Regency.

Pliens, J. David. "Why Do You Hide Your Face? Divine Silence and Speech in the Book of Job." Interpretation. 48:3 (1994, July): 229-238.

Potok , Chain. 1967. The Chosen. New York: Ballantine Books.

Richardson, Jane Marie. "Silence," Religion and Intellectual Life. 21 (Winter, 1987): 49-56.

Roth, John K and Berenbaum, Michael eds. 1989. Holocaust: Religious and Philosophical Implications. First Edition. New York: Paragon House.

Roth, John K. "The Silence of God." Faith and Philosophy. 1:4 (October 1984): 407-418.

Rudy, Henry L. 1981. The Message of Revelation: An Exposition of the Book of Revelation. Volume 2. College Place, WA: Color Press.

Runel, Martin. 1994. Out of Silence: A Journey into Language. New York: H. Holt.

Russel, Jeffery Burton. 1997. A History of Heaven: The Singing Silence. Princeton, NJ: Princeton University Press.

Schapp, James Calvin. 1995, In the Silence There are Ghosts. Grand Rapids, MI.: Baker Books.

Schmidt, Roger. 1988, edition, Exploring Religion. Belmont, Calif.: Wadsworth Press.

Scourfield, J.D.H. "A Note on Jerome's Homily on the Rich Man and Lazarus." The Journal of Theological Studies. 48 (1997, October): 536-539.

Seiss, J.A. 1981. The Apocalypse Lectures on the Book of Revelation. Grand Rapids, MI: Zondervan.

Shea, William. (1981). "The Investigative Judgment of Judah, Ezekiel 1-10," Studies in The Sanctuary and the Atonement, Biblical, Historical and Theological, Edited by A. Wallenkampf and W. R. Lesher. Washington, D.C. Review and Herald.

Sitchin, Zecharia.1992. The Stairway to Heaven. Santa Fe, NM: Bear & Co.

Smith, David B.1991. Heaven. Hagerstown, MD: Review and Herald Pub.

Sobino, Jon. 1978. Christology at the Crossroads. New York: Obris.

Stephens, W. P. 1986. The Theology of Hulrych Zwingli. Oxford: The Clarendon Press.

Straight, Michael Whitney. 1983. After the Long Silence. Thorndike, ME: Thorndike Press.

Strand, Kenneth. 1992. "Foundational Principles of Interpretation." In Symposium on Revelation, Book II. Edited by Frank Holbrook. Silver Spring, MD: Biblical Research Institute, General Conference of Seventh-day Adventists.

Stuhlmueller, Carrol. "Psalm 22: The Deaf and Silent God of Mysticism and Liturgy," Biblical Theology Bulletin. 12 (1982, July): 86-90.

Swedenborg, Emmanuel. 1867, Heaven and Its Wonders and Hell. Philadelphia: J.B. Lippincott & Co.

Sweet, J. M. P. (1997). Revelation. Philadelphia: Westminster Press.

Teaban, John F. 1981, "The Place of Silence in Thomas Merton's Life and Thought." The Message of Thomas Merton. Edited by Patrick Hart. Spencer, MA: Cisterian Pub.

Terrien, Samuel. 1978, The Elusive Presence. New York: Harper and Row .

"The Long Silence." Http://www.wsite, com/Cool20180s3.html.

The Analytical Greek Lexicon. 1967, Grand Rapids, MI: Zondervan.

The Church Hymnal: Official Hymnal of the Seventh-day Adventist Church. 1941, Takoma Park, Washington D.C: Review and Herald.

Thielike, Helmut. 1962. The Silence of God. Grand Rapids, MI: Wm. B. Eerdmans.

______. 1959, Theology of Culture. New York: Oxford University Press.

______ (1956), The Religious Situation. Translated by H. Richard Niebuhr. New York: World.

Vardy, Peter. 1990, The Puzzle of Evil. London: Harper Collins.

Walsh, Jerome T. 1996, Berit Olam: Studies in Hebrew Narrative and Poetry. Collegeville, MN.: The Liturgical Press.

Walvoord, John F. and Roy B. Zuck, Editors. 1983, The Bible Knowledge Commentary. Vol. 2. USA: Victor Books.

Washington, James M. 1986. A Testament of Hope: The Essential Writings and Speeches of Martin Luther King, Jr. New York: Harper.

Watson, Duane.1992, "Babylon," The Anchor Bible Dictionary. New York: Doubleday.

Weems, Renita J. 1999. Listening For God: A Minister's Journey Though Silence and Doubt. New York: Simon & Schuster.

White, Ellen.1940 edition. Desire of Ages. Oakland, CA: Pacific Press.

White, Ellen. (1999 compilation), Christ Triumphant. Hagerstown, MD: Review & Herald.

Wiley, Ralph. 1991, Why Black People Tend to Shout: Cold Facts and Wry Views From a Black Man's World. New York: Carol Publishing Group.

Wilson, William "Righteous," Wilson's Old Testament Word Studies. McLean, VA.: Mac Donald Publishing Co.

Winfrey, Oprah. "Heavenly Body?" US News and World Report. Vol. 122, (March 31, 1997): 18.

Wickes, Thomas. 1851, An Exposition of the Apocalypse. New York: M. W. Dodd.

Wordsworth, C. H. R. 1852, Third Edition. Lectures on the Apocalypse. London, England: Gilbert and Rivington.

Wright, G. Ernest. 1952. God Who Acts: Biblical Theology as Recital: Studies in Biblical Theology 8. Chicago: Henry Regnery.

Young, Edward J. 1972. The Book of Isaiah, Vol. 3. Grand Rapids: Wm. B. Eerdmans.

Youngberg, Verlene DeWitt. 1977. The Revelation of Jesus Christ to His People. Keene, TX: Southwestern Color Graphics Press.

To receive additional copies of *Silence in Heaven* return your prepaid order to:

Teach Services
254 Donovan Road
Brushton, New York 12916
518-358-3494

or

D. Robert Kennedy
Unity Research Institute
P.O. Box 554
South Lancaster, MA 01561
Ph. 978-537-0391
Email: DKJune@hotmail.com

We'd love to send you a free catalog of titles we publish
or even hear your thoughts, reactions, criticism,
about things you did or didn't like about this
or any other book we publish.

Just write or call us at:

TEACH Services, Inc.
254 Donovan Road
Brushton, New York 12916-9738
1-800/367-1998

http://www.TEACHServicesInc.com